A SOCIETY THAT BREATHES ONCE A YEAR

A SOCIETY THAT BREATHES *ONCE A YEAR*

Alex Cecchetti

Book Works, 2012

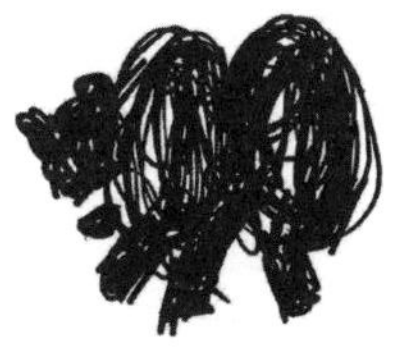

I

— They're all tired.
From the car window he watches the petrol station man walk towards him through puddles of water and oil, cap on his head, face pale as an egg.
— All tired.
Taking the keys from the ignition, he pops the door handle with his elbow and steps out into the cold air. The dawn fog is spread out over the countryside, low and white, so that everything seems lopped off, maimed. The man in the cap pulls out the nozzle with his right hand, makes a half-turn to the left, sticks it in the tank, spits on the ground and leans against the car, pressing the palm of his hand on the cold sheet metal.
— Tired?
— Rough day.
Through the rain-streaked glass you can see all their things, all those things they decided to bring along. Cooking pots, clothing, animal hides, antlers, rags, an axe, and tins of food piled up any which way like a toppling Tower of Babel. And this whole tangled carload of carcasses is covered, mingled, fused together with mud, so it looks like a damp swollen creature made of dirt, leaves and roots.
The man in the cap looks it over, then spits on the ground, takes out the nozzle, wipes it on a greasy rag, makes a half-turn to

ght and puts everything away, the nozzle in the pump and the rag in his back pocket.

— That'll be fifty.

Jerzy stands there motionless, his eyes glued to the mouth of the man in front of him.

— Fifty.

Jerzy jerks around as if someone has called him, somewhere far off across the road, beyond the fog-pale trees. Fifty, the man in the cap repeats. Jerzy's hands are sheathed in rabbit-fur gloves, sewn together with the guts of some unknown animal, and he uses these false paws to rummage in the pockets of his long green canvas trenchcoat. He finds the yellow plastic bag, pries its double knot open with his teeth, and pulls out the money. He counts it with thick, hairy fingers, the unfamiliar faces, the smell of ink.

— Ten heads of men, three women and two old ladies.

Jerzy holds out the money.

— If only they were slaves.

The filling station man rubs his hands on the greasy rag, sticks it under his arm, takes the money, counts it twice between thumb and forefinger, then stuffs it in his jacket, wipes his hands again on the rag, spits on the ground once more and goes back to the shed. You should build a hut so that at least the old ladies can sleep there, Jerzy says behind him, men and women always find a bed. The shed door slams, the clouds above are grey and travel slowly, heavy and silent, all in the same direction.

The asphalt road that runs up through the conifers is covered with damp earth, tangled roots, small animal carcasses with blackened fur. The sun is an elusive blot in a pressure-charged sky, barometric fluctuations giving off a scent of rain.

She is still asleep, head propped against a cushion, wrapped in a grey wool blanket, seat tilted back, breath fogging the window in a slow rhythm. She hasn't seen the man in the cap, she hasn't seen the fog or felt the electricity in the air. As he drives, he runs a hand though her still-damp hair, doing this as if he didn't have the right.

— Just sleep now.

What's the point of telling someone to sleep when they're already
sleeping?
     — That guy could switch his brain off and still stick everything
     in the right hole.
What's the point of talking to someone who's asleep?

— Sara is that you? My God, Sara, are you OK? Where are you?
Sara is that you?

— We're coming back.

The earth itself was made of water, mud dragging everything with it, tree trunks as big as cows, severed rodent heads whirling in the eddies. In the woods she had even seen an animal foetus floating inside a deflated balloon, a being still alien to the world in its transparent flesh. All of this was impossible to describe now amid the reek of meat and potatoes, the flashing lights and the chill of the damp, starless night.

— We're coming back, we're fine, there's been too much rain. Nobody uses pay phones anymore; this one is as dingy as the sky. Sara is holding the blanket still wrapped around her with one hand, the other grips the receiver like a circus trapeze. The voice on the other end just weeps and weeps, and that weeping has now joined the flow of mud, the cracking of trees and the black wind that drones on in her head. Her eyes fixed on the puddle at her feet, she nudges it like so, and five, fifteen circles break up the face reflected there.

A man comes out onto the patio, cupping his hands to light the cigarette between his lips. The white cloud of breath and tobacco rises into the air and falls, pale under the neon lights like the ghost of a roebuck that the wind crushes to the ground with one blow.

— I'm fine, really, everything's fine. We still have the car and
    the money. Yes, I'm fine.

She hangs up, gazes into the puddle at her feet, brushes her hair aside
with one hand and goes up to the man, looking as pale as his smoke.

— Got some tobacco?

Around them it has started raining again. The man raises his fur
hood, runs a hand through his long, thin hair, and takes the package
out of his big jacket, its cloth as black and glossy as crude oil. She
takes the cigarette, holds it to her lips and the man lights it, cupping
his hands. The brief flame lights her whole face up for a moment,
from beneath.

— Going to be like this all week.

She turns towards the rain beating down on the road. Taking a drag
of the cigarette, she holds it in her lungs till her eyes sting, then opens
her mouth and lets the wind slip in and snatch the smoke out of her
throat.

— Further north it's brought down whole mountains.

— We're getting out of here.

Sara turns so that her back is to the road; from there she can see into
the pub through its large, fogged-over windows. Inside are men as
big as trees, women with apelike shoulders, huge heads flat as chairs.
She takes another drag on the cigarette then flicks it down into the
streaming water.

— My granddad had some tobacco that was a hundred years
    old, all black and rotten, but better than this.

— Things keep getting worse. If you're here to hunt, just stay by
    the road and wait, the water always brings along some big
    game, still fresh.

— We're not here to hunt.

A dog or the ghost of a dog emerges from the darkness, yellow and
pale, sopping wet, the fur on its belly black with blood. Slowly,
hesitantly, it edges into the even yellower light of the neon signs.
It's scraggy, with listless red eyes, a dull white bone sticking out of
its swollen, hairless flank. Fucking dog, says the tobacco man.

The dog circles halfway around the two figures, Sara strains to
look over the man's shoulders, through the windows, further on into

the pub, as if that would somehow put her on the other side where Jerzy is eating, sitting in a real chair, after such a long time, cutting meat like an ordinary person, drinking like an ordinary person, or something.

— We're going home.

— Nobody around here has a home anymore, they glide away
   like boats .

Sara moves towards the pub, the man grabs her arm before she can make it in.

— What's your name?

Pravda, she says, and pushes her way inside, pulling her whole arm in behind her along with the yellow dog at her heels.

In the heat of the pub the dog gives off an even stronger reek of beast, like sodden goat; it moves even more hesitantly among the men and women who have lost their homes, eaten up their livestock. Some have been digging in the water for days and don't even know where to bury the bodies they fish out, because the cemetery, they are told, is now a swimming pool. The tobacco man walks by the dog, now standing motionless in the middle of the passage, and aims a kick at its head; yelping, it rolls under a table. Someone else chases it out, pulling the tables away; people are getting to their feet and the dog skids on its curved claws, yelps even louder and trots limping toward the dark end of the pub. The men in the back give it a few more kicks and so it staggers back into the light, foam spraying from its mouth. Someone opens the door again and the dog goes out the way an unwelcome guest would go out with words still stuck in his throat. In the rain beating down on the car park, its legs give way and it collapses into a puddle, head half submerged, gripped by spasms. The hot steam of its breath rises into the air at an ever-slower rhythm, and the wind sweeps away the wisps of fog like fleeing snakes.

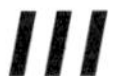

They set off again at night, into the rain that barricades the road
and melts the mountainsides into streams of mud, forced to
keep creeping forward at such a slow pace that from a distance their
headlights look like the lights of a still house in the countryside.
The rain hammers against the windscreen, and all Jerzy can make
out is a kaleidoscope of silvery creatures that wrestle, break
apart, and devour each other before being swept away by gusts
of wind. A wall, a shed, a window, the whole ghost of a house appears
in the glare of the headlights. The car approaches slowly as if
pulling into harbour. Sara starts rummaging through the mudpile
in the backseat, thrusting her hands into it, her arms, her whole head,
working her way into the heap of wet clothes and rotting hides,
roots, cooking pots and leaves. She re-emerges with a filthy shotgun.
Opening the breech, she sticks in a shirt tail, stuffs the cloth all
the way inside using a branch, and when it comes out the other end it
looks like animal dung. She hunts in her jacket and finds a few
cartridges, loads it, snaps the breech shut and puts the gun between
her legs.
— Planning to kill somebody?
These are the first words he's said to her in days. And naturally the
first words, the very first, would have to be a question.
They park the vehicle in the carport by the garage, the rain
beats down on the sheet metal and seems intent on breaking through

and washing everything away, the roof, the house, the hides,
everything, thum thum, thum thum.

 — Why didn't you do anything?

 — When?

 — You know when.

 — Those were people itching to kick somebody, it was us or
the dog.

 — You don't leave someone there to die in agony, you shoot
them.

As they speak the fog of their breath covers their faces, like a mask.
The house is cold and damp and dark. He clicks the dead light
switch, two, three times. Clambering over wooden planks, rags,
a broken chair, he comes back out into the garage where their car is.
He searches through the mudpile they carry with them until he
finds an electric torch. Over by a pile of door and window frames in
one corner, he sees a bear, its shaggy shoulders vast and dark, its
head stuck into the planks and debris, thick forelegs shuffling everything around like empty paper cut-outs. Jerzy falls back against
the staircase and scrambles up it on his hands and knees. He shoves
the planks up against the door, pushes a big table against it and
a chair and when he finds an old bed base he props that against it too,
then shines his torch into the darkness. The two of them pass
through rooms in which the rain pours through the roof like one of
those mountain waterfalls, cascading to the floor and flowing off
somewhere, down through some hole. They make a bed in the bath-
room, using whatever they find. They light a fire in the tub, using
whatever they find, and Jerzy would like to go back to the car and get
an animal pelt, because there's no better way of staying warm than
to slip inside someone else's body. From the window comes an icy
blast of air that makes a noise like the air in a canebrake, or in the nostrils of a goose. Whooooooooo. The tub glows red-hot, the fire in it
casting boat-like shadows.

 When she falls asleep he takes the shotgun out of her clenched
arms. He unlocks the bolt, opens the breech and takes out two
cartridges. Slipping them into his pocket, he snaps the gun shut and
puts it back in her arms.

The bear comes into the room and sits down next to him. Its eyes red from the gleam of the fire, the bear says:

— Good idea.

— What?

— The fire in the tub.

— If you throw a stone in the water, see? It makes circles. Even the rain makes circles in the water. But fire, fire makes circles out of men. Fire is horizontal. It puts men in a circle, without giving any orders except for light, for heat. The circles made by fire are perfect circles.

— How many men can sit around a single fire? a fire is a family, that means seven. Any bigger and a fire would no longer be horizontal, it would be a rite, it would be vertical. The society of men does not need fire, it needs heat separate from light and light separate from heat.

—Look at the stars, don't you see how they put the whole universe in circles?

— Ellipses.

— What.

— The universe moves in ellipses, parabolas, periods. You move farther away, then closer. You don't know squat about geometry.

The bear scratches its shoulder.

— You should swap your silly circle for the more complex image of a ball of string.

In the morning they wake up arse- and shoulder-deep in ice-cold water. The bathtub is black with soot, and the ashes have formed patterns like grey mountains all over its ceramic surface. They strip naked, he rekindles the fire in the tub, burning pieces of a chair he salvaged the night before. They hang their clothes on a line, then like two plucked birds, thin and pale, they huddle on the edge of the tub to dry off, their faces to the fire, growing redder and redder.

— I'm hungry.

— I'll go look in the car, we still have a few things.

— It's not raining.

— No.

— We can travel all day and get there tomorrow.

— Yes maybe.

— What are you thinking about? Don't think about it.

With her bare feet she draws five little figures in a row climbing up one of the many hills of ash.

The city is shining in the full light of morning. Every pane of glass,
every shopfront is a shard of sky and on the street the sheet metal of
the automobiles sends white reflections bright as daytime stars
whirling and flying away from their windows like a fairground ride
and Sara turns her head and narrows her eyes trying to hold onto
those dazzling images a little longer. An old man with teeth of gold,
two boys kindling coals, a man with three white dogs, the faces in
the glass, the girl running through the grass, hips curved like river
bends, the man sleeping in the street under a pile of quilts over
the hot air vent, his beard and hair that float up in the air whenever
the train passes below. The girl spitting on the ground, the mufflers,
hats, jackets, the hands stuffed into pockets. Someone kicking
down a door, someone wielding a bat, I'll kill you, you fucking prat,
faces reddening, people rushing, along the river shore under the
bridge the water racing, foamy grey or foam like cream. The stories
of a city are just one, the night just one, the streets just one, the
houses one by one at the end of tunnels tunnelled by the blind.
The sun shines down on this whole jumble of people and jangle of
metal, faded harrowed faces that go home and go to work, that
stand in queues all staring down, that trudge up stairs and underneath the ground. Fornicators, dictators without throngs, dogs
without their fangs, rodents, pregnant girls, prodigious accidents,
the force of will that pushes on in vain. How will you ever find out

who stole your man? Who is your enemy when your job is gone?
Who is to blame for this whole shitty life? The bank, the state,
the marching multitude. The city has done away with adversaries,
and all it offers now is your ineptitude. That's what Sara thinks.

— I'm lost.

— No, we're almost there, turn here then go straight to the end.

— We're going round in circles.

— Don't you think I know where my mother lives?

— I'm telling you we've been going in circles for a while now.
When they get out of the car they look like two dead bears, or two
rodents, dark and thin with hair pasted to their heads, purple hands,
black swollen fingers. The mud creature that once inhabited their
car is now just dry, cracked earth. Sara looks at the cold sun high in
the cloudless sky, shades her face with one hand, and strains
unsuccessfully to see all the way up here, where we are watching.

I see my mother give birth to steel
And fire
Give birth to children burning in the water
And as columns of smoke dim my vision now
In the dark mist of birth
I am blind
But I plant my feet on the first warm damp clump of earth

PROLOGUE
IN THE FORM OF A ROAD

Jerzy had promised Sara a piece of land, big enough to build a house, and far enough away from other houses to start a new family, something that had never been done before. We'll make new people, he told her. They'd spent a year without getting out of bed except for work, or to go for a Chinese when it wasn't raining out. Jerzy kept promising land, and Sara children, but every time he came it was on her breasts or thighs, or in between her toes. She'd say, if you have land that's all you need, I'll catch fish in the river and you'll club them on the head, then I'll shoot whatever moves and you'll skin it, gut it and we'll boil each piece in water till the meat falls off the bones. And we can put potatoes in the ground, and roots, and in the trees we'll hunt for nests, and suck eggs in the summer and ice in the winter. And your hands will get so big from all the work that even a single finger, this one right here, will be as thick as your cock. And then I won't care which you take me with when you're tired. Sara had talked to her friends about the new family that was in the works and they said that was wonderful, that was really wonderful. And then came the clashes in the streets, with the police burning police cars, the students robbing students. And then the blows to the head, spittle in the face, people mocked, locked up two days, and the radio, the nation's press all shocked, for whatever reason they concocted. And then back to work, back to school, the battle had been fought, the war already lost. And Jerzy said this is shite, there's no enemy to fight. And Sara hadn't done a thing, she said she was right-wing. And from far away the economic crisis flung open the stables of farmers on their uppers, and members of the middle class who couldn't afford to feed their horses. And so they turned the animals out of the barns, and the evicted horses went running along the motorways, across flyovers, through frozen meadows with cold earth that won't even harbour roots. Iron earth for horses that never had to use their teeth before, not even in the mud. Bent to eat snow under a sky that hung lower and lower. And volunteers went out to shoot the lame, wounded, exhausted, emaciated animals. Thirty-two calibre for sure, Sara said. They could eat them, she added.

Horses are dumped in the street only by people who don't understand, who haven't got a clue, Sara continued. We sit and watch what's done by the men in power, we try to understand the global economy, but we're just wasting time. We spend our time reading, trying to figure out a world we never built. We look at the stars, we name constellations, but these are our houses, our lives. If they feel like they belong to other people it's because the men in power make our laws and our complex bureaucracies. They have the time, they own the time, and they use it to create reality. What's reality? This seemingly meaningless maze we inhabit and struggle like fools to understand, instead of building it. There ought to be volunteers who come and shoot us before the wrong season catches us sleeping in ditches. And that was enough to make Jerzy feel like he was surrounded. There was nothing to be done except go back to the land. But what land would be far enough away? No matter where we go we'll have acroplanes and satellites flying overhead, Jerzy said. We may not see them, but they'll be taking pictures of everything, down to the last hair on your arse. You can't live in another society inside another society. It's not like boxes you can stack inside each other. It would be like putting this chair right in the spot where that table is too. Both things at the same time in the same place, it isn't possible.

But she insisted, without lending it too much weight, that two things could easily exist in the same place, materially appear at the same time, occupying the same inch, just as a road is also a journey, or a rabbit can keep running with a piece of buckshot inside. No need to make a big deal out of it, she said, it's like a woman with a child in her belly, or an egg inside a snake. It's not true that each thing has its place, nor that each thing has its time; everything can happen here and now. Boom went Sara clapping her hands. Boom Boom.

And so there wasn't much you could do except find some land, buy it, steal it, far away from everything and set your back to the sun building walls, joining planks, sawing windows. Buying land is a bourgeois thing to do said Jerzy, stealing it is for monarchists Sara answered, giving the state the ultimate right is like cutting something off and then forgetting what. Then when they found out how much land cost, they wondered for days what all those people were still doing in the city. Sara's mother put in a nice fat sum, as she called it, and Jerzy sold the little flat in the centre where he had lived for years as a student. Sara went on a trip out of town and he said he would go to stay with Watt and at Watt's he ran into some other old friends and they wound up in a bar and Jerzy said if you can build a frigging dollhouse that's all you need to know, you just need bigger pieces and you can put your wife in it, your kid, a frigging dog, and they wound up in another bar and Jerzy said he knew how to build a toilet where the shit fell in a bucket and then you could mix it with ashes and let it ferment and then use it to grow potatoes, and it really seemed like that night would never end, and Jerzy was convinced that a house had to have at least two rooms and a door, so that when you're in one room you don't know what's going on in the other. They went from bar to bar like pilgrims, till Jerzy wound up in a bed he'd never seen before, with a girl he'd never seen before, and took a shower when he woke up with the morning already over. And as he spat hot water out of his mouth onto his feet, he thought how he could go on that way forever, going out and fucking different women every time. The alcohol made his head spin, his stomach churn, but he would go out into the low afternoon sun, have a cup of coffee and then set to work rounding up the others for another night out like the last. In any case his cock was bigger than a finger, bigger than a hand, the transformation would take years. Or else he would have to put his hands in the earth, and that would be the first time. He would make a house somewhere far away, a thing you do just once, each person has their own thing, for him that thing was a house. He left without kissing anybody, no point in that when what he wanted was to leave no traces behind, at most a mask, something that wasn't him, something like the dry skin of a snake.

He took another shower when he got to Watt's, then kept washing his hands for three days in a row, six times a day, but before going to pick Sara up at the airport he ended up soaking his left hand in bleach. Every time he could remember, it was his left hand that always smelled of pussy when he'd been with a girl. And every time there was nothing to be done, the smell of pussy lingered for days, for weeks. This made him think that women mark things, take them, exist more than men do, more than dogs, or cats, or any animal he knew.

That night, watching Sara sleep, Jerzy explained this left hand business to himself. It was simple, after all. In bed, if you sleep on your left side, your heart is crushed by everything on the right. How much does your right arm weigh? Your shoulder, chest, a lung full of air? Touching a woman while lying on your left side meant touching her with your right hand, but Jerzy was sure this prevents an erection. He explained it to himself by saying that the heart, when crushed on the left, doesn't have the space and strength to beat as it should. So he turned over on his right, and this seemed to work pretty well, his heart felt lighter, and the fact that he was touching Sara with his left hand confirmed the whole theory. But then he started thinking about the blood flowing from his heart straight to his cock, and started thinking about his sex full of blood, swollen thin as a balloon, and his heart beating hard, too hard, and the balloon filling up, and so he gave up and went to sleep. He knew all he needed to know about balloons.

They had a car and now they also had a trailer, and Jerzy had taken a house apart and packed it up inside. They'd bought the land so far away that it had taken him three days to get there and two weeks to look it over. When he came back with the deed he said he'd signed it on a stone with the wind ruffling the pages, and so they'd put other stones on top of the papers on top of the stone, and that made him think.

It took months but then they left one day at dawn, and for the whole trip Jerzy kept telling himself that in the end making a house was like making a box. He focused on the box, imagining it from the outside and then from the inside. He thought about all the boxes he'd ever seen, chose the best ones and set to turning them round in his head.

Spring had just arrived and the wind, the earth, the metal of the car, Sara's skin, everything gave off the warmth of the season. They drove through military camps that looked abandoned, into a gorge between two mountains that the sun never touched, and the same day they drove through tunnels completed only after years of hard work, driving through them like the wind, in seconds, none of it seemed to make any sense, like the way they went up mountains while all the rivers came down.

When they got there the sun was hot, they felt it on their thighs and cheeks, it made their pupils tiny and their irises yellow. They got out of the car and looked at the fallow field in front of them, the earth was wet, the grass high, they walked into it until they came to a rocky slope, their breath still fogged, but the winter was gone. When they got to the top they looked around, there was still a good bit of field, and then a sort of forest, with trees, shrubs and brambles, things that stand up to the wind and to the weight of the snow. Meanwhile the ground gave off a scent of sperm, Jerzy said, or mildew. Sitting on a rock, Sara stretched her legs out in the air, my feet are sopping wet, she said, is there a road to where we're going?

They went back to the car, Sara took off her shoes, wrung out her wool socks, Jerzy started the engine and they drove down the road but it took them further away instead of closer. With the whole trailer and their chopped-up house in tow, they went back a few miles, tried another road, but that one decided to go down instead of up, then they looked for junctions, detours, anything shaped like an X or Y. A flock of dark birds flecked the sky. Jerzy was sure there had to be a road somewhere. Sara took the map of their property out of the glove compartment, there's no road, she said. They stopped and looked at the map, if that orange thing with nothing on it was their land, then it had no roads. There was a certain logic to this; after all, they had bought a piece of land, not a road. You don't think anyone is going to bother marking everything down on a map, said Jerzy, a map never tells the whole truth. They went back to the fallow field, a little lake of weeds under the warm sun, Jerzy fixed his eyes on it, jerked the wheel around and drove in, leaving the road behind.

When the sun began to graze the peaks of the mountains, the car was still out in the middle of the field, in the tall grass, its wheels stuck in muddy ruts. We should have deflated the tyres, Jerzy gasped as he pushed, his shoulders wedged against the rear bumper, deflating the tyres distributes the weight over a greater surface area, he said, and then his hands went white and all the blood shot into his face in hundreds of red speckles. It's a question of surface area, like with snowshoes, dromedary hooves, or else it'll take another car with four-wheel drive or else we stay here and wait for summer, and as he said all of this and kept pushing the sun slipped behind the mountains and dusk fell. They had unhooked the tarp-covered trailer, but at this point the car was going nowhere. They had bought a piece of land miles away from anything, they would have to make their way across a field, a forest of trees and brambles, and God knows what else. They got out blankets and a big sheet of plastic and slept in the car. In the morning there were two rangers knocking on the windows, they showed their papers, the rangers said they'd need a helicopter to get there, the couple said they'd pull it off, and the officers called a tow truck and got the vehicle back on the road, Jerzy signed a check and paid a fine, Sara made coffee on a camping stove she got from the car. The officers wanted to make sure the matter was settled, what do you plan on doing now, they asked. We'll go down and get a helicopter, they replied. Later on they hid the car and trailer in a wood a few miles north, packed two bags, Sara took the stove, tarps and the shotgun, Jerzy said the gun could stay in the vehicle, but there was no stopping her. The first time he'd come to see the land, Jerzy had gone a different way, through the field and down the slope, he remembered thinking a car would make it, that there had to be a road somewhere. They walked along and he noted every boulder, every bramble, a splintered tree trunk, a hole in the ground, a burrow, a trickle of water and the big pools with the sky inside. By the time they got to the middle of their piece of land dusk had fallen everywhere. They lit a feeble fire with half the wood still wet, and put the rest to dry and stretched a tarp between two big boughs of some tree whose name they didn't even know. They opened tins, set them in the fire and ate out of them while they were still red hot. That was their land, they'd bought it. They said they'd pulled it off, and passed the vodka back and forth with the icy rim of the bottle cutting their lips. They started stomping on the ground, running around shouting and swigging from the bottle till their blood was so fluid that it rose to the topmost surface of their skin, under the last viscous membrane of their eyes, as if the blood wanted to go even further, spray up into the constellations, spatter the stars that came and went behind the grey clouds that came and went, the whole thing like a sea, an ocean above their heads which were spinning, like boats or bombs, or something else, Jerzy said. And Sara went to get the shotgun, there was no stopping her, and fired a shot in the air that sent her sprawling, and a smell of oil and machinery rose up, like when you hit an iron pole with a hammer for too long, or keep scribbling on a piece of paper with a pencil, or something else, Jerzy said. And the smell crawled straight up into their nostrils like a bug. And Jerzy was sure that from then on he would always have that shotgun bug inside his nose. Sara must have it too, living in her nose for years now, ever since she was a little girl. The bug must be nice and fat by now, Jerzy thought, lodged deep in her flesh, sucking away at little veins, digging in its ever-longer legs. Sara must have some eggs in there too, somewhere in her brain maybe.

They slid inside the little tent without even pitching it, and it flopped around them like a limp membrane. The cold kept Jerzy awake all night and in the morning Sara was the first out of the tent, retching, throwing up the meat and beans which lay there in a puddle on the ground looking just the way they'd found them in the tin. All around, their little camp was like a shipwreck and they were drenched in dew. Sara was shivering so hard it looked like there were two of her. The sun wasn't yet up out of the trees and in the cold, rosy morning light the second Sara, the one who shivered more on one side than the other, split neatly away from the first, and still shivering a bit she went to Jerzy. No, I'm not the soul, she told him, I don't think there is one where I am. Then what are you? Jerzy asked. I'm Sara, at least the Sara who shivers a little more on one side than the other. When we shiver too hard you can see there are two of us, but otherwise, the rest of the time, especially in the summer, it doesn't make much difference and nobody notices. And so Jerzy, for no good reason, set to thinking about the order of the universe. And muddled as the whole thing was, he managed to clear up a few points for himself:

1. Reality is propagated and perceived through a very simple system of waves.

2. We should imagine this system as the surface of two co-existing, transparent, spectral oceans. The two oceans are perfectly identical in nature, and differ only in the movement of their waves: Sara one and Sara two.

3. These are inconsistent oceans, the spectra of oceans. Their individual waves, like their individual storms, do not exist in our spectrum of reality. They exist only when the waves of one ocean meet up in the same space and time with the waves of the other ocean. Then a third ocean appears between the two, a concrete, solid one, there in front of our eyes, for a moment, as a resultant: Sara.

4. This third ocean is our world. Sara, Sara lock stock and barrel.

Sara two, also known as Sara who shivers a little more on one side than the other, said that wasn't really what she meant, but in any case it was too late. The sun had started dappling the meadows and the wood with light, and she stopped shivering and went back to being just one woman, the only true Sara, Jerzy told himself, the only one, and yet for the rest of the day he had a hard time feeling fully convinced.

They sat there in the sun wrapped in grey blankets, Sara boiled some water and poured it in two cups where it turned dark as mud. They perched on a tree trunk or on a moss-cloaked rock. Jerzy found some broken biscuits in the bag. That was their land, they had their breakfast on it, and the sun began to warm his forehead and fingertips.

They went back to the car, which took all morning, Jerzy looked at the trailer wrapped in the blue tarp. He'd packed it the right way, planks then straw, planks then straw, like a hamburger. He'd given the thing some thought and figured out that air is the best insulation there is after egg white. He'd already thought about making a house out of meringue, one egg would be enough to produce a cubic metre. As insulation there was nothing better, but then you'd have to live inside the meringue. Straw was the safest, easiest bet, straw was millions of years old, and that provided a degree of security. They would make the toilet first and then around it a house of wood, straw and air.

Making a house was something he'd thought about, but a road, a road is something you find. A road, all roads, especially country roads made of hard-pack gravel, are there before we come along, they already exist, they start from the piece of asphalt where we are and then continue on, and they're there when we come along. But when we come along, and it doesn't matter how long the road has been there, when we come along it's the first time. The first time someone has passed that way. It's the first time for the road. Jerzy didn't really know what he meant by this, but he felt he was arriving at something significant, something big, and would say it if he could only find the words he needed, he knew what it was, but to search for it, to find it, he would have to crack his head open, cut out his tongue, look in a dictionary under R, or maybe S.

To build a road you need to mark a route, draw a line, as straight as possible, as short as possible. Something that goes from A to B. Bring in excavators, and shovels and hoes, and get rid of everything. The rocks are the least of it, it's the tree trunks, the brambles whose roots stretch down into underground caverns, the snake nests, all the things that leave ditches, open up holes, because you can't just dig a road, you have to fill it in, but what do you use to fill in a road, a ditch? Making a house like a box, building the whole thing around a toilet, sure, he'd thought about that, but a road, a road you can make as straight as you like, there will always be the fate of a curve.

Sara had shut herself in the car, wrapped in two blankets, her forehead poking out the window in the sallow sunlight. The sharp air made her nostrils tremble and she said they would have to bring in excavators, but Jerzy said they would drive the house over the house itself. The sun was at the height we call noon when they started unloading the planks from the trailer. They laid the longest ones out in the field, one after another in two parallel rows, and drove the car over them along with the whole trailer. They'd go fifteen yards at a time, then they'd have to start over. According to Jerzy's calculations they had already gone about ninety yards when Sara got the first cramp in her shoulder, and a hundred and seven when Sara definitively decided that the idea was stupid, but the planks held up and Jerzy carried on by himself all afternoon and all afternoon he looked for Sara in the field without finding her, he called her name beyond the hill, in the direction of the woods but got no reply. When he figured he'd made it two hundred yards he looked for the shotgun and as he imagined it was gone. By evening he was damp with sweat and streaked with mud, having brought the vehicle, trailer and house right up to the edge of the forest. He got in the car and switched on the headlights, shining them against that impenetrable darkness, onto a chaotic succession of tall sturdy tree trunks, heaps of branches on the ground intertwined with brambles and shrubs and mossy rocks. He told himself that he'd think about the trees and all that in the morning. He honked the horn three times, then three more, then decided to try his mobile. Sara's phone rang from underneath the passenger seat. He turned off the headlights and the forest disappeared, he turned them back on and said to himself that the shadows cast by the trees, brambles and even the rocks were not at all the same as before. He turned off the headlights once more, he was sure that the forest would move again. Then he thought that although the earth is round and spins on its axis, that doesn't mean you can expect it to spin like a ball, but he put this idea aside for the morning as well. He took the torch and packed a bag with two tins of beans, some dry rusks, and another bottle of vodka, locked the car and headed into the wood. The day before he had memorised every branch, every stone, every pond, but now he was entering it from a completely different angle. He told himself he would have to draw a map, from the road to the wood, from the wood to the tent. Every rock would be a circle, every tree a triangle, the streams of water would be snakes. He thought about how snakes slither into thickets, warm their blood in the sun on hot stones, and when you pass by they either hide or kill. You can't draw a river as a snake, Jerzy told himself, not unless it's a dangerous river, or a passage somewhere, or something. Maybe the stones shouldn't be circles either, not unless the stones rolled easily like wheels, or spheres. Triangles for the trees might do fine, on the other hand. He told himself that the trees were women, all his many women, and found one slender enough to give it a name. Camilla. On the map Camilla would be a three-pointed bar, one point for each branch. By the time he got to the pools of water with the sky in them he had decided a lot of other things about his map, but then he remembered that after the pools came two trees leaning against each other and further on he would come to the big hole in the ground and then a fallen tree and so he put aside the idea of the map.

The light of a fire cast all the shadows of the forest against him, he turned off his torch and hid behind the fallen tree. A few yards from the fire, a rabbit was hung up by its hind legs on a big branch. Using a knife, Sara cut two rings around its back paws, then tugged down on the two lips of skin, the rabbit's pelt rolled back a bit to reveal the raw muscle. Sara held the rabbit's legs apart and made two lengthwise cuts along the inside of each thigh all the way to its sex. She pulled the skin on each side until it came off the muscles and cut it free with a single slice where the tissue clung. It was like watching someone take the trousers off a child. There was no blood, nothing. Jerzy saw all of this from behind the fallen tree, and the rabbit had its back to him, so when Sara cut off the animal's sex, Jerzy saw only her face, an expressionless face. He was sure that if he had been there, she would have said urgh. Sara pulled off the skin; it turned inside out like a glove or something. On the inside the skin was mottled with small reddish blotches, Sara wrapped one end of the pelt around her fist and gave it a few jerks until the skin bunched around the rabbit's head, then she pulled the front legs out just like you would slip off the sleeves of a jacket, then gripped the fur and gave two tugs, then three, and the animal was naked, naked back, neck, ears, mouth, naked eyes. Sara wiped her forehead with the back of her hand, then threw the rabbit skin in a bucket. The two of them pitched the tent, set up camp, a place for the fire and a place for the water. Jerzy impaled the rabbit on a nice straight branch, maybe one of Camilla's branches, he told himself. There had to be other Camillas around, slender, flexible, sturdy, they were good for impaling and roasting things. They propped the rabbit over the fire and fell asleep without even eating it. In the morning the rabbit was gone.

On the third day they made a map, marking circles, triangles and snakes, and drew a darker line straight across the map and called it road number one, then another line that tried to avoid as many triangles as possible. This second line was called road number two. Jerzy had repeatedly checked that there were no Camillas in the way. Sara said that this complicated everything, so Jerzy went into the woods again, and came back with a discovery. A trail that ran through half the forest, the remains of a long-dry creek. They marked every tree that would have to be cut down with a strip of cloth, there were too many for two people to handle. Sara said they would have to call in excavators, hire a tractor, in a day they would have a road wide enough, straight enough, they could make it go wherever they wanted, fill it in with rocks, gravel, it would be a solid road, it would hold up for years, with a drainage ditch or something, and in the end all they'd have to do was give it a name. When they marked the last few trees, they were already close to the pools of water. The sky was mirrored in them and everything around was cold and dark. They circled the pools till the disc of the sun was mirrored there as well, and maybe they thought this would make the experience more pleasant, they stripped naked thin as dogs and got in. The water was cold, the bottom slimy and the smell was definitely a pond smell. Before long they got out again, naked in the cold and dark with pale skin and red bramble marks on their arms and legs. Their limbs started to shiver and their teeth to chatter, they wrapped their clothes around them and still chilled they climbed up the slope. Sara had four ankles and maybe under the folds of the shirt draped over her shoulders there were four breasts, four nipples, two of them further to the left.

There must a rabbit somewhere, a skinless rabbit, Jerzy thought, a rabbit hidden in the shadows somewhere in the wood, a creature sensitive to light and to cold. Eyeballs dangling from their sockets, it would see everything as if from a swing. The bared nerves would react to every change in temperature, every breath of wind, a single leaf, a single branch, a single bramble brushing against it would send spasms of pain flashing through the rabbit's little brain strong enough to knock it out, kill it, a crazed rabbit staggering through the woods. Then he remembered that the rabbit was half cooked, so he told himself there must be a dog somewhere, or maybe a wolf, or if luck would have it, something even bigger.

Jerzy had brought along some boards and made a raft or something to put on the ground and they'd anchored the tent on top. They had dug a latrine twenty yards from the camp and cleaned out one of the ponds. Higher up they found some bushes that gave off a scent like the wind, or something like mint, or something like cut grass. After bathing in the pools, they wrapped themselves in one of the wool blankets and climbed up to where the bushes were; Jerzy rubbed his beard on them, Sara her hair. They called the bushes nipples of the moss god, or kisses of the moss god, then just nipples because they were round. They called the pools the arse of the moss god because sometimes the water was foul, or mouths of the moss god, then just pools or mouths or else eyes, but only when the sky was mirrored in them, or the clouds or other things like that which rarely happened. On their map they had marked down almost all the triangles and circles and snakes in the vicinity. They had also drawn a box that they called their house and now they said that their map was the best map ever made because you could draw the future on it with great precision.

After they'd eaten up all the tins of beans, the dried beef, the coffee, the potatoes, and only after kneading the last bit of flour with water to form a soft white bread to cook over the fire, only then did Sara head into the woods again, gun and all and Jerzy too. They came back without having caught anything, without having shot at anything, they were sure that the whole rabbit business had just been an hallucination.

The rabbits were funny things too. They'd be there and then they'd be gone and to shoot them you had to aim at the feet, never at the head, because it's never where you think it is, and is never as big as you think. And even if you aim at the feet, they're never where you see them, they're where you think you'll see them an instant later, and it's not a question of the future, it's a question of circles. Rabbits go in circles Sara said, they don't know how to run in a straight line because they spend more time in the air than on the ground and when Jerzy saw one he realised that they don't jump or fly either, they stay in orbit like satellites. That's why there's no point in going after them, Sara said, you just wait for them to come back. Even if you know a rabbit's circle it can always vanish, you see it running in front of you and then it's gone, ducking down a hole, an underground passage or something. If there was a difference between a hare and a rabbit it was more than just the ears. Hares run, rabbits vanish underground without a trace, not even their droppings, since they eat them, and so as far as Jerzy knew there might even be just one rabbit in the whole world, a sort of fuzzy monster that goes in circles pretending to be many when it's just the only one. And only when they finished the vodka as well did Jerzy decide to go back to the car. They had left some provisions in the car, and there were other things in the trailer that could be useful. How many days had gone by, how many weeks? They might have spent years bathing in the pools, Jerzy couldn't say for sure. Then it crossed his mind that winter hadn't come yet nor summer either and so he mentally added up the tins of meat and vegetables they had emptied, the beer and vodka, and came to the conclusion that the gap in his memory was a few days long, no more. When they got to the car it looked like a hallucination, a shining object, alien and yet warm, familiar. He felt like it might start talking, or flee like an animal, or just sit there motionless forever, like a house or a stone. He walked around it the way you walk around a big dead animal or an accident scene. The door of the car was wide open, the window smashed, the padding of Sara's seat had been ripped out with deep vertical slashes in the upholstery. The bags had been opened, torn apart, the preserves and tins had been split in half and there was nothing left inside. Their clothes were scattered all around the car for yards, along with bits of plastic, cardboard, empty, shredded packets of dry biscuits. When they got back to the camp they had enough to last them for two days, or maybe three, Sara said. There was no more milk, just a piece of salted meat.

When you walk around with a gun in your hand it's because you're hungry. It doesn't matter what your food is that day, said Sara, it might even be revenge, or something else but it's still hunger. If you walk around with a gun in your hand it's because you're hungry but that doesn't make you a hunter. To be a hunter you have to entrust your hunger to one eye, just one. Sara moved behind the fire, its red glow lit her from beneath, she raised an arm up against the night and made a little fist, her hand reflecting the light of the flames, a second tiny moon. This is a rabbit, she said, it doesn't matter if you only see a hand, this is a rabbit and you have just one eye, which eye would you rather have? Which eye would you never want gouged out? Sara picked up a stick and held it in the fire until it was red hot. It would be better for you to have just one eye. Jerzy shut one eye, any which one, and saw a rabbit or a fist. Sara told him to throw a stone straight at the rabbit, and the stone vanished into the night. To know which eye sees a rabbit instead of a fist you have to look through the right hole, said Sara. Now stretch your arms out in front of you, put your hands together and make a little cunt, holding it right in front of you. Look through the hole at the rabbit with both eyes, keep it in the little cunt. Sara stood there with her fist still raised in the air and told Jerzy to move the cunt slowly toward his face, keeping the rabbit in the hole, she said that only one eye was really watching the rabbit, the other was looking somewhere else, watching something else, God knows what. What? Jerzy asked. And just then the tent crashed to the ground and sprang back up like a bow when an arrow is fired. And the sound it made was like the wind tugging at sails or when you snap a big sheet in the air or something. And Sara disappeared, and the fire in Jerzy's eyes went out and the darkness was everywhere and its breathing was hard and hoarse. Sara shouted out from somewhere that there was an animal, Jerzy grabbed the shotgun and pointed it at the darkness, at the point where the darkness was even darker, even glossier. The tent gave another jerk, pieces of metal flew into the air, falling into the coals where they sent up sparks and began to turn red, and somewhere strings kept dully vibrating and something started crawling across the ground, sweeping away the rocks, the branches, creeping along the bushes, and all around the darkness was breathing so hard now that you couldn't imagine its size. The tent had been sort of sucked away from the ground, along with the light of the fire, for good. Silence fell suddenly, unexpected. In this new era of darkness and man with no shelter or fire, the gun barrel still challenged the empty air in front of it and Jerzy's arms were starting to hurt, tears were streaming down his cheeks and under his chin and he was beginning to feel seriously hungry. Which eye should you close when there's nothing to see?

When they came down the mountain road the frost had not yet melted into drops of dew. Faces pale, wrapped in mud-streaked blankets. They came down perpendicular to the road which instead was all tight sharp turns, like a twisted snake. The sky was low and grey, the clouds piled up quick and dark and seemed guided by some impulse, as if they were all trying to converge somewhere. They came down a bluff, sliding on their behinds, and when they got to the bottom they no longer had any desire to get up; they rolled belly-down and lay there like fallen soldiers, chests pressed against the low grass, heads hanging in the void of another bluff even further below. They saw dark clouds swirling somewhere in the sky, swallowing each other up, they lifted their heads and rolled their eyes up until they could see only clouds, no grass and no trees and no earth, only quick, dark clouds, till they got dizzy. Jerzy had a question in his stomach or somewhere like that. What did the other eye see when the other eye saw a rabbit? Sara went on pretending to be dead for a bit, then said that she really didn't know, those are things nobody teaches you, she said.

It was evening by the time they got to the trunk road, a van took them to a junction where there was a sign saying that somewhere in that direction they would find some houses stuck together, a village, a square, or something. The face of the guy in the van was the first face they'd seen in days. They looked at him the way you look at a foreign country. When the van dropped them off, it started raining fat drops of warm rain, the leaves of the trees bent down under their weight, the grass too. They saw snails slithering among ripples and rivulets along the side of the road, shells white as bone against the dark green of the dank countryside.

They found lodging in a house run by an old lady who wore her hair in a bun at the nape of her neck so it looked like she had two heads. Jerzy thought that she must have a mouth there under the hair, two eyes, a nose, the head of her Siamese twin or something. They took a hot bath in a cracked tub, the water was so blistering that Jerzy said it was like being stewed over a fire. Then he turned his head and saw his own face in the mirror on the wall, but there was something wrong: he moved an arm but the figure in the mirror moved a shoulder, he ran a hand through his hair but the figure on the other side splashed hot water on its face, then he realised that it was Sara's face in the mirror, and so he wondered when he had started to think he was Sara, that he had Sara's face. Sara pulled her hair back, put her feet up on the edge of the tub and said it must have been a wolf, or a bear, or a man, something big and strong enough to pull the tent up off its stakes, drag it away with everything inside, through the brambles and bushes. It must have smelled the dried beef from afar, perhaps catching the scent from miles away. Perhaps it was the same thing that had stolen the rabbit from the fire, a fox? Were there foxes around there? Jerzy didn't know squat about foxes or wolves. Perhaps it was the same thing that had ripped the car door off its hinges, gutted Sara's seat, devoured their food.

Jerzy said they'd been talking about this for hours, maybe the second head hidden in the old lady's hair could tell them something. And what if it had been a chasm of nothingness making its way through the wood? A piece of the void that sucked in everything around it. Something that invalidated causes, eradicated their link to effects. If nothingness exists it can't be seen, if nothingness exists why shouldn't it be a movement? A fox would have slipped into the tent and back out without making such a commotion, Sara said. Jerzy couldn't remember what part of the camp he'd ended up in with the shotgun. When had he picked it up? Sara didn't know. Jerzy said that to be a hunter you should always know where your gun is. Sara said maybe that was true, maybe she wasn't a hunter, maybe she wasn't cut out for this whole thing at all. They got up from the bath, standing in the hot steam, Sara had a purple mark, tumefied blood clustered under the skin, all the way from her white ribs to her thin, pale left arm. She said yes, it hurt. They got into bed. Jerzy held Sara in his arms as she cried. He had wanted to ask her something earlier when they were still in the bathtub, stewing their skin off, now it was too late, maybe even a little too late to ask her tomorrow, still there was one thing Jerzy really didn't get, couldn't explain to himself, what had become of Sara when the tent lifted up off the ground? Where had she hidden?

Where had she vanished to? Though if he had the same face as Sara, maybe it didn't matter in the end.

They were sure that the old lady had a little head or a little sister hidden under her hair, maybe that was who she was talking to in the hallways lit by smudgy windows, in the morning as she laid the tables, brought the coffee. Her daughter was already just as old but invisible, and when she appeared she was a sort of smile and a pair of eyeglasses. The guests were people passing through, headed from that region to the next, none stayed more than one night, everyone moved on except the two of them, and this must have been a favourite topic of conversation for the head in the hair and her sister the old lady. There was a garden and iron chairs painted pale pink, there was also a pool with three frogs or three toads in it and there was a corner where the sun lingered until evening. When the toads were singing you couldn't see them, when they weren't singing they sat on the floating leaves or motionless in the water. If you picked them up they sang, but if they sang while you were holding them it didn't matter anymore, the toad, the song, nothing. Just the clammy, slimy body, rough against your fingers, a fragile and repulsive and silly form of life. Jerzy told Sara that if you picked up a toad all you could do was torture it, but there were people who sucked the warts on their backs, the same people who talked to saints, who saw the devil and talked to the dead. Sara said she would like to talk with the dead. What for? To ask them how they are. They aren't, Jerzy said, they simply aren't. He said it without believing it, he said it just because it sounded good. It went well with his face that day and the toad in his hands. The dead would be pissed off at him, he would apologise some other day.

The man was wearing a green camouflage suit and had brought along a tiny double, a boy with the same face and the same clothes. It was evening when they arrived, and both Jerzy and Sara thought that the two clones were going to war or something. The child ate everything without chewing, he would choke someday, long before he got hair in his armpits. The man said it was a bear that wreaked all that havoc, he'd seen one rip the door off an SUV and throw it three yards the way we'd crumple up paper or toss away litter. The man mimed throwing his sandwich in the air, he did it like a slow-motion replay. Bam, he said. Bears rummage everywhere, carry everything off, they do it with a degree of calm, from a distance they look like kids turning a cube over in their hands. They put everything in their mouths, all they do is eat. The man in the green camo was convinced, it was a bear, and they were lucky even to be there listening to him answer all their questions. You could have lost an arm, an eye, it could have fractured your sternum with a single caress, bang, like that boom and then crushed your skull on the ground crack, till your brain squirted out your nose squish, popped out your eyes splat, then it would have played a little more with your head on the ground ding-da-ling before gobbling you up, or else you would have had to shoot it right in the forehead bam but it takes them close to a minute sometimes two to figure out they're dead. The man and his boy clone were coming back from a hunting trip, an initiation. They had stripped the skins off the animals, cut them into pieces severing the bones at the joints, and put everything into two big blue cool-boxes. Jerzy asked what they had shot, they said rabbits. Rabbits? And some other big thing with fur, antlers, a roebuck, a deer, something big like that. The boy was chattering away after his father, his mouth crammed full of food, and Jerzy stared into it. That hole plugged with saliva-moistened bread, rotting baby teeth, a green, swollen tongue, that hole was the locus of the word, the musical instrument of the ape dynasty. It was the same as talking out of your arse. He thought of the applause and renown garnered throughout Europe and America by masters of the stage who enthralled an entire century by talking out of their arse, farting words with their buttocks. In the end, talking was a matter of dividing the air, compressing it and making body parts, organs, cartilage vibrate. What were the vocal cords but bands of bone covered in viscous membranes? In the end, eating was just like singing. It was easy to get the two mixed up, they went through the same hole, why should one be more refined than the other? Who says you can't kill a rabbit if you talk out of your arse? In the end wasn't it meat that was vibrating? Even the cartilage resembling rabbit bones? The line of thought suggested by the boy's mouth led to enormously significant conclusions, too much for him to assimilate in just one day. Then like everyone who goes hunting and has ever gutted a fish, skinned a squirrel or slaughtered a goat, even on a single occasion, they started to talk about civil war. If a civil war breaks out, they said, hoping.

Jerzy went to the loo, and as he opened the door, the old lady appeared in the hallway with her back to him, pausing by the mirror to fix her hair, and Jerzy clearly saw that hidden under her hair was another head, a nose, a mouth, two eyes, a face identical to the old lady's face reflected in the mirror. The head told him that there was nothing to be done but to go back, he had to go back.

They cut through the field, then as the head in the old lady's hair had said to do, they crossed under the trunk road by following a stream under a bridge, climbed back up onto the road and found themselves standing before the entrance to a big supermarket. They counted twenty-seven sections, with aisles full of tins, bottles, yoghurt, milk, eggs, water, beer. The meat was cut, ground, wrapped, vacuum-packed. Pieces of thigh and flank, ground, minced, and pounded cuts of meat were laid out over nineteen yards in the refrigerated section. Where did they kill all those animals? Where did they come from? How many supermarkets were out there with twenty-seven sections and nineteen-yard-long refrigerators full of meat? And no one was in this one, just the two of them wandering around with a metal trolley meant to be filled up with things that didn't belong to them yet, at least not until they decided to take them outside, past the checkout, and pay for them. They could have scampered around with a full trolley for an hour, two hours, without buying anything. Touching everything and owning nothing, Jerzy said, not bad.

You'll go hunting with the shotgun, and strip the skin off rabbits when I'm not around. If it really turns your stomach, then I'll take care of clubbing the fish on the head, and the deer as well, if there are deer. I'll go looking for toads in the pools, and if I find any I'll pick them up and lick their warts until the dead decide to talk to us about how they are, what they do. The bears are hungry, but they keep both eyes wide open, what do they know about hunters needing to be one-eyed? What do they know about the dead, about the void, about how you build a road or a house? They would teach the bears to roll up the metal shutters of supermarkets, bam, and the bears would go sliding and skating all through the poultry section, all the way to the crates of eggs, squish squish, all they had to do was band together into groups, gangs, come down the mountains, yum yum, they would teach the bears to light a fire, zip zap, and cook, chop chop. The bears would let them scratch their backs, pick their teeth, who says you can only ride horses? Some people ride ostriches, Sara said.

The old red Cherokee dropped them off by the side of the road right in front of the muddy field. The man said there was a river further down that was big enough for bears to fish in, but he hadn't seen any bears, but there had to be some, sure as there are fish in the river and men on the roads. He had seen a fox, two foxes, and a third one he caught in a trap while looking for a wolf. There were wolves around, but you didn't often see them either. In any case foxes aren't any craftier than wolves if they get caught in a steel trap without even any snow to hide it. Whatever the two of them wanted to do with their scanty piece of land they'd have to do it before winter, long before, said the man in the red Cherokee, come to think of it, before autumn.

The trailer still had the green plastic tarp around it, though Jerzy seemed to remember it being a different colour; it was warm under the sun and the iron cables and ropes that held it all wrapped up hadn't moved a bit. The whole thing could hold up for years, men or educated bears would be able to build a house with it someday, after the great nuclear wars, when the world would just be a gob of cold grey ash. The car sat there with its wheels on two planks. White, gleaming, it too warm under the midday sun. Sara saw the shredded, gutted seat, the door still open. Inside was a wasp, or a bee, something yellow that buzzed around and sometimes disappeared into the gap between the steering wheel and the dash, or behind the windscreen. Maybe the whole vehicle had become a wasp's nest. If the wasps got organised they could all beat their tissue-paper wings in unison, lift the car up and send it crashing back to the ground. What would be the point of that? Jerzy asked himself. The idea was really stupid, why should the wasps do that to their nest? The thing that troubled him was that his brain had thought of it anyhow, of self-destruction, self-humiliation.

They had brought along two big bags from the supermarket containing meat, eggs, milk, flour, tinned beans and vodka. They put in some still-intact clothes that were drying on the grass, they put in a hammer, nails, a red metal can, they took the plastic tarp that Jerzy wanted to wrap around their shit to turn it into fertiliser, then burdened like a couple of mules they headed into the woods again.

Sara dragged her bag along the ground leaving a trail stripped clean of leaves, of moss, if it were damp you'd think it was the track of some giant snail, Jerzy said. They reached the pools, Jerzy took a box out of his green raincoat and emptied the bodies of three toads into what they called the arsehole of the moss god, because in the heat the pools reeked even more. The toads lay where they fell, maybe they were discussing what to do, maybe they were dead. Sara threw a stone at them and they vanished, swimming towards the tree roots that stretched down into the water.

Their camp lay there motionless the way corpses lie motionless. The tent was jammed in a bush, as if someone or something had tried to pull it all the way through. The longer Jerzy looked at it, the more he thought it resembled a tumour. One part of the tent was completely swallowed up by the twisted brambles, the other lay there looking bulgy, maybe the mattress was still in there, some tins, maybe it had filled up with water after the rain. A pool of water had formed on the boards, gnats were hovering over it like a column of dust in a ray of light. Amid the blackened remains of the fire they could see some stakes and hooks. They lifted up the raft made of planks and let the water drain away, leaned the platform against a tree and then stood there looking at the tent. Sara picked up a stick and took a thwack at the bulgy part. Jerzy said the tent was pregnant, Sara said there might be a snake in there. Jerzy said that snakes live in the jungle, or in books, maybe there was water in there. They kicked it a few times, then touched it with their hands, Sara shrieked that there was something moving inside. They pulled the tent out, opened it while the sun was still up, the water drained away like off a horse's rump, carrying along a few dry leaves and a piece of damp, green, mouldy bread. They laid the tent out to dry, hoisted up the sodden mattress and hung it over two branches. They made a fire, and put the dry meat, the eggs, and all the food they wouldn't be eating into a waterproof bag and hung it up in a tree, fifteen or twenty yards from the campsite. Jerzy said he could hear the toads singing.

Make a road before autumn, make a house before autumn, or something, wasn't that what the man in the red Cherokee said? Or maybe it was the head hidden in the old lady's hair who said it? Carrying the planks on his back through the forest would be a killer, and then there were the panes of glass he wanted to use for windows, and above all the tool chest. He mentally reviewed the contents of the tool chest. There were definitely some long iron nails, there was an axe because he remembered putting it in, there were the heads of a spade, a pitchfork and a pick. He had bought them the day before they left in a huge store packed with hundreds of customers, men and women, and he walked around with the head of a pick in his hands and thought about how he could crack open all those men's and women's heads if he only wanted to. Smash the tiny ribcage of the baby parked in that carrycot by the checkout. Things that are possible have a certain allure, and that possibility made him feel like a murderer, made him feel guilty, so he was forced to lower his eyes and almost cradle the pick in his arms like a child. The tool chest above all, also contained a chainsaw.

Sara was crouched in the tall grass with the sun not yet up, just a purple glow hinting at the dawn. Behind her was the forest, in front of her an expanse of low-hanging mist bathed the countryside. Jerzy looked at her eyes, then looked at the open space in front of them. Sara rolled her head all the way around and let out a deep breath. Jerzy stretched out with his back on the ground, the grass was cold, damp, squelchy and so he tried to get up but Sara told him to keep still. In that position Jerzy's arse would soon be soaking wet and his spine frozen stiff. He could see Sara's gun, her nose, two eyes, a patch of forehead and hair, and right behind her hair the purple sky, which was turn-ing pink. Then under his ribcage, there on the ground, he felt some-thing else, a sort of thump thump, Jerzy thought it was his heart, the way he'd hear it in his ears before falling asleep, thump thump, or feel it hot in his teeth when they ached. Thump thump, he looked at Sara, she was staring straight ahead, thump thump, and lifting her arm slowly with the whole of the gun, thump thump, Jerzy lay there with his back on the ground, the sky dappling itself with pale blue. Sara was hold-ing the gun straight in front of her, her left eye closed and her right eye trained along the barrel. Two holes lined up like two planets, somewhere soon there would be an eclipse, Jerzy was sure of it, but he couldn't see a thing from where he was lying, hold on Sara said. Jerzy only stared into the hole of her pupil, he imagined it piercing her eyes, her skull all the way to her brain, and just as easily he could imagine the light pouring into it, but how this light could become an image was something he couldn't explain to himself, and above all at what point, where? Thump thump thrump, now he heard two hearts, now three overlapping, crisscrossed, they were weaving some plot above the fog. Thump thump thu-thump-thrump, hold on. Sara's pupil was motionless, with no change in diameter, like a mouth, then it said BOOM. The sound of the gun compressed the air in his ears, her shoulder jerked back, her head was motionless, Jerzy was sure Sara was gone, shot out of her pupil, there was nothing left of her. Maybe she had followed the shot, maybe they had crashed down somewhere together, maybe she hadn't even fired, there was no need. Then the smell of graphite slipped into his nostrils straight up to where the shotgun bug was burrowed in, getting fat. Shit, shit, said Sara, shit.

They were bent over looking at the earth, the trampled grass, little patches of water they called tracks, they followed the prints, then lost them somewhere, then found them again, they followed them into a wood, then told themselves they weren't the same tracks as before, then followed every bent bush, every broken leaf, every branch out of place and there are a lot of branches out of place in a wood. They paused in front of an upturned stone, with a brown worm writhing in the spot where it had been pressing down. Someone had flipped that stone over, they were sure of it. They looked at the size of the stone, they looked at the worm. No, it couldn't have been the worm, maybe a sudden rotational acceleration of the planet.

It was something with antlers, a short tail, something with fur, and there were two or three of that something. They stood on four legs, with a head that moved only up or down, they definitely weren't rabbits. They won't be back tomorrow, let's wait three days, if they don't come back we'll wait three more, said Sara. Why three days? According to Sara animals had no memory. Jerzy said that even wood had a memory, even glass, and as a result this had to extend to plants, what's the sense in believing that animals didn't have one? All the more reason to come back after three days, said Sara, let them think we were just passing through.

Make a road before autumn, make a house before autumn. Jerzy was sure it was the man in the red Cherokee who had said that. That man's face was a blind smudge in his memory, but he could still hear his voice, he felt like it was right there next to him reminding him to act, to do something, something specific, simple, but that absolutely had to be done before autumn. The map was now a snarl of symbols, there were circles, triangles, forks, there were three toads in three spots, and inside the spots next to the toads there was also a moon and stars. By their house they had drawn a little square hanging right over a triangle, and then there were snakes and two-tailed snakes and in the margins they had drawn two hearts a big one and a little one. They had already shot at the hearts and they'd fled, so they attached the hearts to arrows that went in three different directions. On the map Jerzy had also traced the dry streambed that ran through the woods almost all the way to their camp. Wide enough, straight enough, a true embryo of a road.

Cutting down a tree was a breeze, he'd make two notches in the trunk a few inches deep, one parallel to the ground, one at a forty-five degree angle like a smile, and that smile would look in the direction where the tree was supposed to fall. Then he could start sawing it in two from the other side. A cut deep enough to go through the whole trunk, but not all the way, just two or three fingerbreadths before going through the smile. Now the tree was a door, the trunk rising up into the canopy was held together only by a thin hinge of wood fibre and live sap, an empire on tiptoe. All it would take was a little wind, a tug on a rope or a wedge hammered into the notch, driven deep in until the definitive crack. The tree would fall, a few branches snapping off, if there were birds they would rise up in flight, the foliage would rub together, he would look at all that devastation and wipe his forehead with the back of his hand or something.

Sara shot rabbits, he skinned and cleaned them. It was a thing he'd never done before, but he made each cut with precision, first the hind paws then along the thighs and then, if the rabbit was male, he sliced its balls off, just as he'd seen her do one night very long ago.

There were no questions to ask, no doubts, one hand held the knife steady, the other tugged the skin down, there was nothing else to be said about it, they could have cut his tongue out, thrown it to the dogs, he still could have taught anyone to skin a rabbit. You only had to see a thing once to get the knack of it. Understanding it was a different matter, but the action pierced the pupil, slid into every nerve, all the way to the wrists, the fingers, passing through the shoulders. There was nothing to be said. He stuck an index finger into the rabbit's armpit between the raw muscle and the skin and zipp pulled out the naked leg the way you'd take off a shirt sleeve. Skinning a rabbit he could do, it was shooting one that he found impossible. It wasn't so much a question of being blind, one-eyed, cyclopic, the shooting eye had nothing to do with it. What he found impossible was arresting any kind of movement. He didn't have it in him to stop something that was running, let alone the flight of a lark, a crow, or any other kind of bird. Stopping something in the air means that then the thing falls, Jerzy said, we'll never know where it was going.

Every three days they would get up before dawn, for how long now they couldn't say, you'd have to count every time the sun had come up behind the hill, every time they'd fallen asleep in the tall, coarse grass, every time that they shot and missed, or that they got a rabbit. They'll be back Sara said, but Jerzy was convinced that the animals might not know the three-day rule, maybe they ought to have come back the next day, why hadn't they ever tried in the evening? If they're animals they'll be thirsty, Jerzy said, we should look for a river, lie in wait by the pools, ask the toads.

By the time Jerzy found the river they had walked all morning in the direction indicated by the man in the red Cherokee. The current and the rocks turned the water into a white foam that swirled in greyer areas, and grew calmer only towards the banks, where dead leaves and branches rotted, floating in slow circles. Further down the river must be tamer, or maybe further up there was a pool, something like a lake with fish in it. Sara said that further down, the river was a river of mud and further up a trickle, or a puddle, or just more foam and if there were fish they were all dead already with their heads smashed against the rocks.

Jerzy went down along the bank, following the current, the river ran between tall, oval rocks and was much more precipitous. He was forced to go back into the wood, amid the moss and damp stones with trees clinging to them, their roots encircling the slippery rock. He followed the river, saw it disappear and reappear through the dark tree trunks, black interludes between one image of light and the next, then a tree trunk moved and slid down into the water. Jerzy stopped and took a closer look, the tree was gliding upstream, now it had a shoulder, now it had a head, and when the trunk reared up on something like two thick legs, he immediately concluded it was not a tree.

The bear moved slowly in the distance, its wide back and powerful behind swaying hypnotically. Jerzy stood there watching the dark bulk of it. The sound of the river against the rocks, the water forming eddies and the eddies burbling at the uneven rhythm beaten by the rock, by the carp or salmon and the powerful thighs of the bear that kept unevenly beating the rhythm. Jerzy watched without seeing anymore, listened without hearing anymore, his eyes on the huge buttocks and his ears aimed at the water and the wind in the leaves that was saying something too, but Jerzy couldn't catch what. And all these sounds and above all the bear's behind that kept swaying at the same rhythm, and the chirr chirr of some cicada and the tock tock of a broken branch knocking in the wind and maybe the glimmers of light from the river piercing the wood, all these things snatched his thoughts away, filled his mind, emptied his gaze.

Jerzy stood there like an idiot, a thin, pale lunatic staring at the bear's behind as it swayed without coming any closer without moving back. This is my best trick, said the bear. Jerzy heard this voice behind him, behind his left shoulder somewhere, but the bear's arse was still down in the river swaying. If you want my protection now you must eat my diseases and suckle from my breast, but I never fall ill and have no milk to give, said the bear. The voice that Jerzy heard over his left shoulder was familiar to him, he was acquainted with it, but the voice said it was the bear and this confused him, he tried to think about turning his head, looking in that direction, but the powerful arse, down in the river, was swaying so perfectly that he could not move at all or even look away.

The glimmers from the river piercing the wood created waves of light that settled from time to time on Jerzy's face. He walked inside those glimmers like a fish, his mouth open his eyes dark-ringed, his legs pushing him forward. He reached the river with a dry throat, a burning mouth. He crouched down over the water and started drinking from his hands. The riverbed was limpid, transparent, little pebbles with moist eyes, and from the crests of the water the sun shot white arrows at his irises and into his pupils. He found himself in the river with the water up to his chest, freezing his legs and gnawing at his sex. He moved forwards with the current pushing him downstream, and chilled and pale he reached the other shore. He went up the river along the bank, bent by the weight of his sodden clothes. The bear's behind fishing in the eddies, then nothing, then there it was again swaying irresistibly. Jerzy fell onto his back, opened his eyes and now the river had taken the place of the sky and down below the leaves on the trees carried the shadow of the sun at different intensities, not like the walls of a house but as only trees can do. The shadow was green, or dark, or light like a temperature, colder, warmer.

He went further up the river, the rocks became whiter and smoother, round and polished. The river was now a fountain of white foam, the water was crashing against the rocks, swirling around, fishing silt from the bottom and coming up grey. There must be dead carcasses under there, imprisoned for ever by the motion of the current, forced to float up and down like in hell, bones doomed to strike against the rock, crack and shatter, until they become sand that would settle on a lake shore somewhere. On the other bank of the river, under the afternoon sun Sara was bathing her ankles and feet, and wiping her cool hand over her forehead and neck. He saw her without being seen and knew that something would happen, that soon there would be two of her, if she would only put her legs into the icy water, if a cloud could only come over the sun. Jerzy prayed to the trees to cast cold shadows on her shoulders, he asked the river to chill her wrists. All these prayers and Sara's ankles, all this anticipation and her shoulders too made Jerzy stretch out on a rock, smooth, pale, and round. Sara looked up and saw him on the other side of the river, his eyes on her, his hands and belly pressed against the rock, she said nothing and did not greet him with a smile but kept pouring water over her feet and ankles, behind her knees and inside her thighs until the skin started to tremble and its thin blond fuzz stood on end. From time to time her eyes darted to watch him, his hands clutching the rock, his stomach, his belly, his sex rubbing against it. Every muscle, every tendon in Jerzy's body was taking part in a movement that was ever less ambiguous and ever more obvious. If the wind were only colder, if the sun would only lengthen the shadows, I would see you walk out of her skin on your own two legs.

Jerzy didn't recognise any of these rocks, any of these trees, there were no Camillas and that meant that they were either lost or very far away. His clothes were still damp and the evening air would soon chill them. Sara was asking to stop and rest more and more often and the stops were longer and longer. They came into a clearing and saw black wires swaying in the sky, the electricity pylon stood in the middle of it like a tower or a sentinel, or a marching soldier. They walked towards it until they were right underneath, the pylon rising up over them, a structure of steel beams that cut the sky into dark diamonds and silvery triangles. They sat down in the middle and listened to the wires go zzzzzz zzzzzzz up in the air.

We don't need to make a road, making a road is like going out of the house but taking the house along with you. Jerzy took the bottle of vodka out of the bag. It's like at the supermarket, if you go out the door with this thing in your hands, you haven't gone out the door at all. If all these things keep coming all the way here along with us, how can we say we're really here? He took a long swig then passed the vodka to Sara. This is something the bear told you? Jerzy had no doubt in his mind that the bear had spoken, just what it said he couldn't say, because of the magnificent behind that ensnared all his thoughts, but this was more or less the gist of it, or something. The bear also said that if Sara killed animals, then he would have to find a way to bring animals back into the wood. Jerzy pointed out the introduction of the three toads, you don't shoot toads, the bear said, then nothing else, not even its behind wallowing in the river, nothing. After that came the rock but Jerzy didn't say this.

He took another long swig of vodka, pulled off his still-damp shirt and trousers and climbed up the pylon. The steel was hot where the sun fell on it, and ice-cold in the shade. The sun was turning pink to the west and more and more purple to the east. He stopped halfway up, clinging like a skinned monkey. The wires ran through a wood to another pylon that emerged a few yards over the branches, beyond it he could see some houses, or maybe just some lights. The evening air had something familiar about it, a bit of smoke, a howling dog. Down below Sara was hugging her legs to her chest. What do you see? Our camp, Jerzy replied, it must be over there, and stretching his bare arm out into the emptiness he pointed to a wood that rose up on a hill.

They slept in a hole in the ground covered in leaves, in the morning they swept away the traces of the fire from the night before and set off towards the tent again. Jerzy told her the dream he had in the hole in the ground. They had painted some trees red, but he couldn't remember why. One of these trees had two knots in it, two deep, dark hollows that looked like eyes and then the big red head with black eyes started talking to him. Jerzy couldn't remember its exact words just the gist of it, and the gist of it was a threat, something terrible was going to happen. Then the canopy of the tree broke right off and soared up into the sky, and from the trunk a column of thick black smoke rose into the air to form the shape of a tail, like the tail of a monkey or something. The tail tried to grab Jerzy and he tried to get away as best he could. When the tail grabbed him by the legs, Jerzy clung to a tree trunk. The more the tail tightened and pulled, the harder he hung on. And so, in the voice of dreams the tail told him, I wanted to catch you but you caught yourself, so much the better. And then Jerzy realised he was clinging to the tree that the tail grew out of and now he couldn't let go. But the sense of danger had passed, and a feeling of peace or even joy crept inside him. Jerzy told all this to Sara as they were walking back, and he ran and jumped and clung to the tree trunks and tugged on hanging boughs. Sara, on the other hand, had dreamed that she was walking along the river bank, and suddenly noticed she was carrying a great weight in her arms, something heavy yet fragile, something tender that she did not want to part with, not at all. Strangely, she couldn't bend her neck or head or even her eyes, so the soft weight did not have a name, a body, or an image. Then the thing began to move and touch her breast, and so Sara knew the way you know things in dreams that the weight was her child. She also knew that if she looked at it, the child would turn into water and flow away to mingle with the water of the river. So the goal of her journey was to carry her child to safety, away from the river or maybe back to its source or down to its mouth, but to do this she must never look down at him, or maybe it was a her. Along the river she ran into Jerzy and Jerzy looked stern or maybe angry and he asked her what she was dong with a stranger's child in her arms. Surprised and confused, she looked down, and her child turned into water and slipped away into the river. Sara could have told him this dream, had she only remembered it.

They'd found a river to draw as a snake, they made it twistier at the top, curling up at the bottom and in a corner of the map they drew three viper heads. Right in the middle of the snake they drew eddies as spirals, and then next to the eddies they added a big rock, this time drawn just like a circle and lower down, inside the snake, Jerzy made a black scribble, like two skeins of wool tangled up together or two planets colliding, captured in a single picture the moment before they explode and devastate a whole system of ellipses, or simply two flies fucking in the air, Jerzy said. Sara asked if that scribble was the bear and Jerzy said it was. On the map, the snake and their camp were not as close together as they remembered, and in that area lower down towards the edge of the page Jerzy added a star-shaped figure, or rather a star-shaped tower. We should try to avoid the star, Jerzy said, fine said Sara.

Cleaning your arse with leaves, that was easy and if you know how to make a fire, shoot a rabbit or even crush a walnut, then you also know how to make soap. Those few things, killing, crushing, and burning were all it took. All you had to do was mix the ashes left by a fire in the morning with the oil of a plant or the fat of some animal. Men had discovered this in the summer when the sun kindles dry leaves and destroys forests and they must have found the roasted body of a deer, a fox, a wolf, a rabbit, they gathered the soap like berries, thought Jerzy, or olives, or fish in the river. That aside, it was not the kind of forest where palm fronds can be woven into huts. It had nary a banana tree to take leaves as plates to eat on, or coconuts to cut and use as cups, or cotton plants to make underpants. He thought of natives, naked men with fingers plunged in flour paste. If you can carve out a coconut then you can make a boat, Jerzy was sure of this. People who tumble into gorges and grab onto the branches reach the bottom with their arse sore but a big stick in their hands. And those people are the people who go back to their houses pound their baton on the ground, say that it's a sceptre and march off to war.

Staked out gun and all behind a big fallen tree, Sara said it was stupid to think that man invented things by mistake or that he encountered soap, dogs or sticks by chance. With the gun trained on the warm purple wood of the evening, her impatient eyes seemed to see something as yet invisible, a possibility that already inhabited the space in front of them, like someone imagining an actor's gestures, voice, and monologue when standing before an empty stage in an empty theatre. When you cook you always do it over a fire, and all it takes is a bit of ash on a dirty plate to make soap, the dirtier the plate the more soap you have, there's no need to go looking for a theory of error to explain things like that, Sara said. If someone boils meat in a pot, maybe they'll discover that when the fat runs down into the fire it forms a nasty looking scum and that nasty scum is soap, but then how do you explain the meat boiling in the pot? So Jerzy thought of cavemen hunting deer and thought of deer running away and how as they run they fall into big pools of sulphurous water seething with bubbles, and an exploding geyser that cooks them all of a sudden shooting them up in the air, and a man who says flambé! And then once you've convinced yourself everything happens by mistake, tell me how you explain something as simple as an arrow?

They'd been sitting like that for a while, waiting, and that sitting-doing-nothing was what they called hunting. Building a house means declaring a war, Jerzy thought, on brambles, on rocks, on bears, on the earth. And just then all the things in his head seemed to line up in single file, like a road that you clear through briars and trees, to see everything you weren't able to see. One eye on the foe in case it's on the march, the earth, the leaf, the weed, the larch. The road is the arch of your gaze through the pines, he said to himself, the mountains and the countryside, the grass that keeps growing higher than high. The bend is a doubt that must be cleared, the way up a sword, the way down a snare, and so in his mind the warning followed on of its own accord: if you wander off or stray afar, then sad and harsh is the fate in store. All of this may have had to do with the fact that he and Sara were staked out waiting, or else with all the words that end in ing, so that warning is like threatening. If the wood or the hill heeds the road's beckoning, then along comes the hedgehog or the boar, round the bend into a snare, and black, crushed rot is the fate in store. Toothless and gutless it lies on its flank, the path of the eye has stumbled and blinked. Jerzy looked at Sara who was sitting there motionless, still staring at the wood in front of them. She too had the expression of someone with a tra-la-la stuck in her brain.

Whooooom whooooom, before they saw them coming they heard them, whooom whooom like breaths vibrating inside enormous walls of flesh, whooom whooom and then just the wood, a branch rustling above or another one snapping below and then again whooooom whoooom, as if these deep, distant sounds came from caves inside the earth, inside the wood, and the most incomprehensible thing was that those caves were coming closer, shifting, moving here and there and their echo was following, and it was hard to imagine them with legs, but Jerzy managed. And the caves on legs come forward and were deer, and Sara stood there like an empty puppet behind the gun, then all she said was shhhhh even though what she really wanted to say was that when you are faster than your own arrow, you are already the prey, and killing turns into suicide.

In the end it all crystallised into the great majestic head of an adult buck with antlers so branched that you couldn't tell them apart from the surrounding trees, a figure as big as the wood itself and at the same time small as a pin and with some whooooom whooooms from other bucks and other does who were coming forward slowly, step by step, and their heads dipping down and then up as if in greeting or just to pretend nothing was going on and then again whooooom whooooom and then bang and then a flight and a crash of branches and a moment later nothing. They went to look for the buck, a young male that had gone on running without realising it was already dead. Sara instructed Jerzy on how to cut away the animal's anus, cut off its sex, slip two fingers under the skin of its belly, slide the knife in, open it up and empty it out like a sack.

Rising over the fields were yellow flowers and white flowers and columns of vermillion flowers with their stems covered in baby fuzz, and flowers that were not flowers but something like a soft white star on a hard thin stalk. And Sara picked one and blew on it and a legion of other little stars rose up into the air leaving the stalk bare and Jerzy watched them ride off on the wind and he followed one in particular after singling it out among the rest, and that one rose up and then dipped down and Jerzy's legs had vanished, his arms too, and he followed that flight as if it were him flying and he hoped it would never end. When he lost sight of the star he just sat there as if he had nothing left to say or do, and then he took a leaf from the stalk Sara was holding in her hands and ate it. The leaf was bitter, a bitterness he liked. There were flowers like bunches of grapes, and others shaped like bells hanging from a single stem all in a row one after another and the stem bent under their weight in a sweet, gentle curve, almost a parabola, an ellipse Jerzy thought.

And as they walked the grass in the field, the earth, the flowers and all the rest walked ahead, jumping, trembling, dipping up and down, here and there and so they stopped and the whole field stopped, they looked around, nothing was moving, everything was motionless or at the most the wind made distant trees sway pliantly. They took a step and the field took a step, they ran and everything was running along with them, faster and faster, Jerzy, Sara, the field, and the field always ahead, second-guessing their intentions, their direction. Hundreds of little insects, something like grasshoppers, the same colour as the grass, the same colour as the flowers, and others the same colour as the dry stalks were running jumping scrambling always a step ahead. And when Jerzy and Sara stopped, everything stopped, every bug settled on a stone, clung to a branch, a stem, a dry stalk of grass, or else slipped into the earth, then they took a step and every-thing was in motion again, everything was running and jumping, and it could go on forever without ever changing, making the field run their whole lives long, as long as the field lasted. And Jerzy wasn't thinking about the universe or about the motion of the stars or planets or about what time was or what life was or all those other things, he wouldn't have thought about them even if he'd been able to. Then they made love, with the bugs creeping into their hair and crawling behind their knees and landing on their thighs and Sara had a flower stuck in her bum or maybe it was a stringy purple stalk or maybe a young thistle, but whatever it was she liked it there. She put her hands on Jerzy's arse and held him on top of her until the end. Until he said oh fuck, oh fuck, and even longer.

And then for no specific reason Jerzy began breathing with his whole nose stuck inside Sara's mouth, he couldn't remember when he started maybe it was just because her breath smelled good or maybe because Sara's mouth was just the right size and so he put his nose inside and sometimes his mouth and she asked him to sing a song into it, or just say his name or shout it as if he were in a cave all the way into the depths of her lungs or somewhere down there, but when he shouted in she laughed and had to pull him away from her mouth or she would have choked on that laugh. And one day Jerzy even got two horses, one was chestnut and the other dappled, he never said where he got them but he must have stolen them across the border marked by the star pylon, somewhere over there where the dogs would bark. And they rode the horses until evening, in the wood, over the fields, with their bums sliding on the animals' sweaty backs, and only when the sweat had become a thick white foam did they let them drink by the river and Sara got off her horse and went to the round smooth rock and Jerzy turned away because he recognised it, and then Sara said something. What? The rock. The rock? Do you think it's pregnant? And then Jerzy gave the horses a couple of slaps on the rear and said off you go! Olé! And other things like that, but the horses didn't want to go anywhere, even though Jerzy had read in books that horses always knew the way home, but it wasn't a question of memory or smell or anything like that, you just had to point them in the right direction and slap them on the rear, so Sara said maybe that wasn't the right direction and the horses knew it. And the horses' breath was warm, and they blew it out their noses and that air seemed to come from vast cavities that couldn't possibly fit inside the belly of just one animal, or else a horse was hollow inside down to the knees. They led the horses to a meadow and

Jerzy slapped them on the rear again but they just stood there quietly letting themselves be caressed by the evening breeze, their manes like grass, their coats gleaming, their necks long as giraffes', and they looked funny with those slender legs holding up that big hollow body, and then there was something majestic about their necks and heads, and in their foreheads, and there was something even more ancient in their manes and tails, and Jerzy came to the conclusion that if you can find your way home when you're drunk and then not even remember how you got there in the morning, then a horse can do that too, get drunk and go home. The theory didn't really change what he already knew about horses, but it added a detail that at least to Jerzy seemed important, that the horse, like a drunk, decides for itself when to go home, and this often happens when there's nothing left to drink or when they want you to pay your tab.

Jerzy could no longer remember what they were supposed to make before autumn, a door, a house, or a road, but he'd started to think about primitive men, Neanderthals, all those people who they said lived in caves and let hair grow all over their body and went around brandishing clubs made from bones. The man in the red Cherokee had said something about the autumn, but his voice was no longer so troubling. The bear's arse, on the other hand, was haunting him, he seemed to glimpse it everywhere, round and powerful, in harmony with the birdcalls, the frush frush of the trees and the tick tack of his brain. The real difference between him and the bear, or rather between him and the bear's arse, definitely wasn't the hair. What do we really know about the hair on a Neanderthal? To Jerzy it was clear that hair didn't make the animal, and above all that the scant fuzz of a half-ape wasn't the link between beasts and cavemen. He thought of all the books he had paged through back home, in libraries, the scientific reviews in his dentist's office, all those illustrations of men squatting to hit two rocks together, or dragging deer by the antlers, and wandering through dry yellow prairies, always a bit hunched over, with their legs like so and their knees a little bent, as if they were all crippled, never quite standing up and never quite crouching down, as if cavemen all had haemorrhoids or sciatica or something. What earthly advantage was there to walking like an idiot? The bear had more or less clearly said that the road was a trap, that the road wasn't necessary, and the bear's arse was more present than the voice of the man in the red Cherokee and it was hairier than a caveman. And so he started searching through the wood, and further down towards the river, and further up towards the rocky outcroppings outside the boundaries of his map, Sara would follow him with the gun or fall asleep in a meadow and he kept searching under the roots of twisted trees, in the crevices between stones, or down inside the tunnels of rabbit warrens or foxholes. He was looking for caves and he wanted them to be damp, dark, deep with streams, rivers, and lakes inside, and rooms with such high ceilings that they would turn his voice into the voice of a giant. Caves lit by fluorescent plants, with pale, transparent salamanders running over the stone, their moist eyes like mirrors reflecting the stalagmites and stalactites and the stalamnites or stalactrites and all those other things that go down come up or are smooth and polished as bone. What would they do with a cave anyway? Sara asked and so Jerzy said that as far as he knew there were no bears without caves but that all the ones he'd managed to find were small, dark and full of spiders. He stuck his nose into Sara's mouth and started breathing, then peered into it with one eye, that was Sara's cave, too small for a bear, he stuck his mouth inside and shouted something and Sara started laughing because it tickled her lungs. What Jerzy didn't see was that somewhere deep down she wanted that bear too, maybe to kill it, or just to talk to it the way she wanted to talk to the dead, and that was because she had been traumatised, violated, devastated by a single incident that took place in her childhood. When she was still a little girl, she once left a plastic bag of rubbish on the lawn in front of her house. She left it there rather than dragging it ten more yards and throwing it in the public bin simply because she hated lifting up the lid. Not because the lid was always filthy and sticky so much as because she couldn't stand the humiliation of having to stand on tiptoe to reach it. The next day she got up early, feeling apprehensive and ran out on the lawn. The bag lay on the ground in tatters, lacerated, shredded, with all the rubbish scattered, strewn around for yards. Up to then she had always believed, without devoting much thought to the question, that if things exist and happen they always exist and happen before our eyes, because of us, when we're around. But instead, the thing that had violated her bin bag existed in spite of her and without asking permission.

It was that season, and the animals went to drink at the pools more and more often, and the berries were red and dark and there were trees that bowed down under the weight of wild fruit, or clusters of fish eggs, and the ducks flew down and skidded onto the lake and then the bark of the trees could become a dish and Jerzy had even eaten it once and told himself it was good. And in this whole time of abundance for every tree or a stone, for every fire or a bird but even for the wind they used the word thing. And for cutting, sawing, turning, tightening, stretching, pulling, skinning, ripping, throwing, and sometimes even for killing they used the word thingying. So they would simply say: thingy the thing, or let's thingy the thing, or she'd say I thingied the thing with the thingum, or Jerzy would say the thingy thingummed.

And there were little plants, with green leaves toothed like a dog's growl and they had white flowers with black spots and white flowers with red spots and when you came closer they took flight and then you saw that they weren't flowers but really butterflies. Butterflies with white and grey and red paper wings and purple ones too and they had blue and yellow streaks and there were wings that were just yellow, so yellow that Jerzy asked himself what the colour of the sun really was. And there were flowers where two whole butterflies could fit inside, or else a bee and a butterfly and there were still whiter flowers shaped like fragile oh-so-slender bones or flowers with pink petals wrapped around petals of an even paler pink and still other petals in infinite folds that could hatch armies of bugs, wasps and larvae and caterpillars and transparent grubs, and Jerzy stuck a finger inside and pushed the finger till it went through into the stem, a stringy, hard damp stalk and when he pulled the whole plant out of the ground and looked at it hanging in the air he thought that the dirt-caked, veiny root, branching into a multitude of other tiny roots and shoots and then millions of other fragile pale hairs, more than anything else, resembled him more intimately than a potato, a mandrake or any other little wild turnip penis.

Either you talk to bears or you don't talk to bears, there's no in-between, Jerzy told himself. It's like cavemen, either they stand up straight on two legs or they're crouched down on all fours, one or the other, there's no in-between, OK even a bear can stand up on two legs when it's angry and even a man can get on his knees sometimes. Jerzy tried to remember when and why he would ever have got down on his knees and he couldn't think of anything, anything at all. He wasn't mad, there was no question about that, he wasn't like the people in the parks who go around talking to pigeons, he'd seen lots of those people and they were nothing like him. He didn't talk to the ducks, or to the trees that gave off a smell of piss at night, or the walls or the air, not unless they spoke first. A bear means a cave, there was no more question in Jerzy's mind about that.

So if there had to be lakes inside these caves, he told himself, all you had to do was follow a brook or a river, follow it until it disappeared into the ground inside some sort of hole, and that hole would suck in the rocks, the trees, the fish, a whole bear, even though a bear with an arse like that would plug the whole thing up, Jerzy thought. And one day as he was hunting for caves he found something on a tree, deep marks raking through the bark down into its living heart. Dark, red and lacerated, the gashes seemed to form a horrible tangle, and because the grooves were deep enough to stick a finger in, Jerzy stuck one in and ran it over and around them and the marks began to play him like a turntable and Jerzy heard the tip of his finger trembling, meta-carpus, carpus, ulna, radius, humerus and then every vertebra of his spine, up to the cave of his brain where the tremor became an echo, and that echo was the bear grunting and grunting like a dumb brute and this was quite a letdown. Dumb brute of a bear, thought Jerzy, and then he ran his finger the other way and presto the crude grunts turned into a voice. I know you'll have repeatedly listened to this recording backwards like a moron before finally playing it the right way round, said the bear, and added that there were no caves, that there was no point in looking for them and there was no point in asking himself what he had to do before autumn, because jumpers weren't invented in the summer. Nor is there any point in going to look for other claw-marks like this on trees or stones, because I'd much rather trim my claws than leave messages. Jerzy tried listening to the recordings again and they said the same things in different words, in the end he just figured that even if there were caves the bear certainly wouldn't have told him where. And he got in the habit of always carrying around a long thin piece of cloth ripped from a sheet, torn from a shirt, something that would be useful if he ran across a burrow, a pile of rocks, a dry creek or even just a hole, because caves breathe and if there were any he would see the cloth flap up in the air or else vanish sucked down into the earth. In the winter it would be easier to flush out that bear's arse, wherever the snow had melted without sunshine, under that patch of red or brown earth he would surely find an entrance.

Under the leaves, in the fissures, under the bark, in the water and the pools, down inside the fox droppings and decaying things and amid animal hairs there were eggs, millions of transparent coloured larvae that had been waiting for years and perhaps would go on waiting, and they were all round, oval like when you blow into saliva and bubbles form or like all growing things. And there were spiders as big as your hand with a real taste for bird eggs, and birds with a real taste for spider flesh, and there were toads that came from God knows where that carried eggs on their backs and there had to be birds capable of devouring them with their beaks, or else they would eat the fish, the fish with their mouths full of eggs, their own and the toads', and if man was spawned in some part of the world it had to be inside a mouth like that. And there were bugs that ate corpses and others that ate dark black fruit that grew out of plants that were always damp, and emerald green caterpillars with yellow stripes, or red and furry ones or purple with blue backs and big red dots, and out of their bums or maybe their mouths they drooled something all around like a spider web, and nibbled on leaves and dug tunnels everywhere down inside the trees. Caterpillars like that would never have time to talk, or smoke a pipe, they were too voracious, they would spend all their time eating and shitting out silk. And there were beetles with totemic heads and mucid slugs and fireflies and the fireflies attacked the slugs at night in gangs of three or more and devoured them bite by bite tearing them to shreds under the flashing red lights that came out of their translucent bellies.

Ahead of them all went the dogs, baying as they pretended to be wolves and barking as they also pretended to be dogs, and behind them came the men, he counted twenty or maybe fifteen, because some looked a lot alike, with loose camo suits, green caps, red faces, some had moustaches and then there were some with beards and some with even redder spotty cheeks and they all had shotguns and they all had knives in their belts but they carried bags over their shoulders that were all different colours, green, yellow, orange, silver, fuchsia, and they hiked up through the wood all five or six yards apart and there were some who gave orders and some who didn't understand and Jerzy walked among them, his shoes patched with the hide of some animal and his head in a floppy hat and his thin torso in a jumper with holes in it from woodworms and his fingers blackened by the fire and he had a necklace made from river pebbles and bits of wood that he'd chosen for some unknown reason and from the way he looked at the other men you'd think that he was lost. The trees seemed to slip through the wood and step up to meet the marching host of men, as if the earth were moving and they were standing still. Some fired shots in the air, some fired shots at trees, some fired shots with their mouths, bam bam, these people were sure itching to shoot, Jerzy thought. Then far away the dogs, in the thick of the thickets, set to barking, and then they heard the brambles uprooted and something trampling the ground, splintering the branches until two big dark bodies with lowered snouts came rolling towards them, panting reeking, and the men had no idea what to do. Some started running and some shouted to shoot and so the others shot, some at branches, others at the ground, until one of those dark low beasts broke its neck running and crumpled to the ground rolling for yards, the other veered to the right or maybe to the left and was soon shot down, its dark pelt cloaked in red blood. They went on like that all day, the dogs ahead and them behind, and the beautiful bucks stepped up to meet them as if they wanted at all costs to be killed, and the men left the bodies behind them, lying gracelessly in grotesque poses, and in the evening they lined up the animal carcasses along the dirt road and got out their knives and some explained to others how to gut a boar or a deer and so the men started cutting big chunks of meat from the animals' haunches and sticking their hands into their bellies, and Jerzy walked among them and they cursed and swore and the sacs of deer intestines split open and the air reeked with their stench, and on the ground under the men's boots were rubbery pieces of heart and flaccid stomachs and green sacs that were intestines and blue sacs that might have been kidneys and strings of fat and dark entrails. And those men kept emptying out the animals' bodies and opened up their diaphragms looking for the heart and pulled and tugged. And Jerzy wound up in a photo, next to a heavy-set guy, one of the moustached ones, and between them was a boar or what was left of a boar and before having his picture taken the man had wiped his face with his bloody hand and said something in a language Jerzy didn't know. And then he saw them load the corpses onto truck beds, get into their vans, get into their jeeps, and they asked him if he needed a ride. Where to? Jerzy asked. They left him there in the middle of the road with the carcasses of a deer and a boar, one animal each as agreed, even though he hadn't fired a shot because he didn't have a gun. And when the last jeep went around the curve behind the hill Jerzy looked around and there was just blood and tyre tracks and there were other things, nameless and lifeless. He hoisted the animals onto his shoulders and went into the wood. We're parasites, tumours, drones, ants Sara said, bees, you say? Of course, tiny bugs, devouring everything like locusts, that's what we're capable of, Sara said again. Locusts repeated Jerzy as he tugged at the skin of the deer, there's no difference, none, we're like bacteria, like tumours, worse than rats. Men didn't seem so alien to the world after all, they were made of the same substance, they behaved the same way. If you think about it, Jerzy said, man is the highest expression of the world.

And the slugs went eeeee eeeee all night under the assault of the fireflies and the next day there were once again grasshoppers, locusts rubbing their legs together crah crah on their abdomens and the spiders zrr zrr rubbing too and the beetles trr trr rubbing their heads against their necks or clarck clarck chirring their jaws clack clack grinding their carapace teeth day and night.

The night didn't mean the sun going to die behind the mountains, not at all, he knew that. It was not a phenomenon produced by the black dust of a volcano that erupted every day at the same time, this was also quite clear, but knowing that the night was the effect of the earth's rotation on its axis didn't make much difference. Because if the earth rotates and the sun always illuminates one part of it leaving others progressively in the dark, then night was just a movement, and this was not all that different from saying that the sun goes to die or the night has owl wings and other things like that. And so it seemed to him that it had been quite a huge mistake to give a name to days and not to nights. This and more he set to thinking as the bear went on reviling him, refusing to let him sleep. The insults were horrid and thus also childish, cruel, dumb. It wasn't the words so much as the emotion and tone of the grunting that made him freeze up in terror and forced him into intellectual, scientific, some would say phenomenological retreat. When he tried repeating them to Sara, they had lost their power. You're a dickful of piss. You've got a plug up your arse and that's why such shit comes out your mouth. All you're good for is lapping heifer arse, you nutsack for mule bollocks, you shit eater, pud puller, and above all cocksucker. The cocks in question belonged to snipe, porcupines, horses, giraffes, miscellaneous marsupials, there were the pizzles of hippos and antelopes, the arseholes of various other species especially from North Africa or else Asian ones like pandas. More specifically, what the voice reproached him for was a simple lack of guts and responsibility with regards to the bloodbath perpetrated on his land and around it, a bloodbath that had involved the killing of creatures over which he still had some indefinite right or perhaps mandate. It remained unclear why he ought to suck male genital organs because of this, but it produced a feeling of humiliation; perhaps, Jerzy wondered, it might be easier to take if he were homosexual?

You come here with your little whore to play all primitive and then she's the one shooting, she's the one killing, she's the one cutting off balls, skinning and gutting, come on tell me, does she bugger you too? The bear had never used such crude language before, it must be really pissed off. The beetles on the other hand had a shell as polished as the metal flank of a vehicle, an extremely sophisticated mechanical suit of armour whose language necessarily reflected that chrome-like perfection. Unfortunately the beetles refused to talk, they preferred to dance and glitter. Everything about a beetle had a rhythm, followed a complicated system of compulsive behaviour, and this necessarily added a sacred element, there was something almost religious in repetition, something to which one could not remain indifferent.

You suck beetle dick. You suck dung-beetle dick. And then, of course: you suck panda dick.

All these insults were woven from the sound of guns and animals, and of snails. A bow was quieter, at most a bow might go slint or slitch, although Sara was sure that a bow could hit the note B or some could hit a C, and some bowstrings when well-waxed could hit an A, and it was natural that war had been invented first and later music or else who knows, maybe cavemen went around hunting and singing at the same time.

The lifeless body of a toad floated with its swollen belly sticking out of the water in one of the pools or eyes of the moss god. Its legs were splayed and its head in tatters, nibbled perhaps by some bird or some fish, but Jerzy knew that even grasshoppers and locusts could kill a toad, suck its brain out of its eyes. He lifted it out of the water and skinned it like you'd skin any animal. This demanded great patience and precision. Back at the camp, he carved up the toad carefully severing cutting its joints and boiled each piece in a pot until the meat fell off the bones. He gathered up the bones and ate the meat. He pulled a button off his shirt and used the thread to sew the toadskin into a little pocket, or a little bag, he put the bones inside then closed it up. He walked into the wood, climbed a hill and left the ragged bundle on a little exposed rock. When he came back he had diarrhoea and nausea for three, four days, he said it was the toad singing and it wanted its bones back and wanted its skin back, then he'd laugh and then throw up again.

There was no hospital to go to and if there was there was no road that went there and if there was a road Jerzy wouldn't have wanted to go, over his dead body he said, and Sara looked around and things seemed warm, damp, swarming with tiny lives, busy lives intent on carrying out, with immense obstinacy and utter perfection, the only task they had ever taken into consideration, living. And Jerzy went back and forth between the hammock and the latrine, and sometimes he couldn't make it in time and would shit himself without a shred of dignity. Spruuut and he'd shit himself. And Sara said he looked like he'd been beaten up and Jerzy said that was to be expected when every fart came at him like a punch in the face. And one night after eating some soft pale things and drinking a warm thing that smelled awful Jerzy started staring past the fire, over by a tree and then closed one eye and opened another and then went like so with his eyes and then like so again and Sara said you've got the eyes of a madman and then to play a trick on her he said I can see the dead, I can see ghosts, and there's one over there, stop, hush, behind you, by that tree, and so she got frightened and upset and he felt her looking at him in horror as if he were the ghost, as if the dead man were him. And the next day the same thing, and Sara told him I don't like it when you frighten me but Jerzy didn't understand how you could be frightened of a ghost, wouldn't it be more horrible, more unbearable if he'd seen nothing, absolutely nothing? You told me you wanted to talk to the dead. Yes, but not at night, in the daytime.

The experience allowed him to draw up a personal hygiene list with the first part dedicated to materials he could only imagine like snow, which he considered the most effective method, as it cleans, cools and is suited to anyone's anatomy. He sang the praises of snow so much that he couldn't wait for it to be winter. Sand, had he found any, would have been perfect, it gets off the thickest residue and absorbs even the most liquid substance. On the other hand he had tried every kind of leaf, grass, weeds, moss and he was sure that everything would do fine except nettles, as for the rest you just have to avoid wiping too hard, too forcefully or else splat, your fingers would go through the leaf. Then came pinecones, he had tried them both open and closed, and contrary to all expectations they were effective and pleasant, but nothing was better than water for cleaning one's arse, not even river stones which if found in the sun burned too much and if taken from the icy water burnt just as much or maybe even more. Once he could move around without shitting himself, Jerzy went to peer into the pools, there were tadpoles, little creatures that resembled magnified sperm, with oval heads and long tails. If there was a relationship between the toad puppet and the tadpole it was by way of vomit and diarrhoea, in the end the price of life was not so high.

One day the night caught them unawares, falling suddenly, first there was light then none. They were also caught unawares by the cold and rain and sometimes by clouds that drifted up from the river, from the earth, from the moss. The sunsets grew ever more purple and the dawn broke ever lower and there were almost no shadows anymore, it's all for the best, said Jerzy, they must have left. And then Sara began to test out the future, asking questions about this and that. What will you do if the earth opens up or if the bear comes back? If the river swells in the daytime and overflows at night? Not questions every day or all together, but like the rain that comes every so often and then stays for two days, wets the earth and makes the mushrooms grow, some noxious and swollen with worms, others meaty and broad-crowned, the kind you search for beneath well-rotted leaves or underground. What will you do if my period stops and my belly swells? Where do you grab hold of the child to pull it out and what if its arm breaks, its foot twists and its head is soft? If you throw it in the river they'll find it downstream and come looking up here, because there's never been a child without a mother, and if that's enough for them that's enough to come and kill us. If you dig a hole for the child you'll have a mound that's soft in summer and hard in winter, at night the dog will dig it up and the raven will eat its eyes out in the evening or gobble at its belly in the day, the guts still full of milk. And Jerzy simply said that they would hold the child the way they held a cradle, the way they held a gun, the way you hold a knife in your hand, things she herself had said before. And so Sara threw herself into the future with her hands tied. And if I want to leave, tomorrow, now, tonight? I'll ask you to stay. I won't listen. You'll have to listen. I'll cut my ears off. I'll hold you by the arm. My arm will come off. I'll hold you by the hair. And my hair will rip away and you'll be left holding my scalp. I'll grab you by the feet. And my feet will bite me away. Then it's your legs that I'll hold onto, Jerzy said. And when my legs come off as well in the haste to flee what will you hold me by? By your guts. And when she finally saw herself torn to pieces Sara laughed.

His fingers were not yet as thick as his cock but they had gone hunting, killed fish and eaten eggs stolen from birds' nests in trees, and when Jerzy climbed up there for the first time, the tree felt to him like time or something and up there, with his fingers closing around the speckled egg, he felt closer to the present than ever and when he stuck the egg in the bag and climbed down he had the clear impression that he was going back in time. And so he convinced Sara to climb up one of the tallest trees and stay there for a while, even though it wasn't egg season because all it did was rain. And Sara climbed up to the top and Jerzy got a crick in his neck from watching but then he went to sleep wrapped up in a pelt under the warm sun, and when Sara woke him up he asked how long he'd been asleep, she said three years, well then I didn't dream much. Feeling better? Much better.

Jerzy had also seen himself torn to pieces, it happened at least twice, the last time his nose was in a hole, the knot of a tree, his mouth on the ground eating pine needles. He was afraid but then he started peeking inside his own ears which he could finally see for the first time because they were hung from a branch by a ribbon tied in a bow or something. He saw their labyrinthine shape, their tiny hairs, and a clump of yellow wax, and they were swaying in the wind and so he heard the wind go ffffw ffffw and then he held them against each other and the ears listened to each other like the ocean in a shell whooosh whooosh then he took them off the ribbon and threw one into the wood and the other over by the water and he could hear the crr crr or glug glug and then he wanted to put one around the neck of some animal, but he couldn't find any animals and he couldn't find his ears again either although he kept hearing the rustle of grass somewhere far away and the fish as well. As for his hands, they pushed themselves into the ground like roots and blossomed like shoots. The legs did not belong to him, neither did the arms. He saw the bones come out of the flesh and gather themselves into a heap on the ground and his skin had swollen up like a balloon and held everything together, the ears, the nose, the hands, the bones. As usual he couldn't manage to see his eyes, where on earth had they got to? Jerzy couldn't remember the first time he felt himself torn to pieces, but there must have been a first time. Or else it had been when he discovered geometry while cutting up tomatoes, potatoes or else when he set to torturing the cucumber. He cut the cucumber in half and got two circles, he cut it at an angle and got two ellipses, a pear split in half made a cone, an orange two hemispheres and isosceles triangles, geometry was like speech, it only came along when you had something like a knife in your hand and something else to eat and then that was not the right time for geometry.

And water seeped into the tent at night and kept them awake, and when they got hungry they never managed to die, but there eyes grew keener and their hands gripped tighter, they clutched things, threw them, ripped them, broke them with much more strength and their legs as well. And Jerzy took the knife and carved an S on a piece of wood, he said that it wasn't a river or a snake but a sort of story, something like life, and Sara made coffee from dark dried herbs and said she didn't feel at all like a line or a curve either. Of course not, you have to add a sort of fourth dimension to the S, you pretend it's moving while standing still. And so Sara sat down and asked about death and he started carving a new drawing. Death was in it from the beginning and couldn't be nothingness, if death were nothingness you would have to give nothingness an idea of existence. Jerzy twisted the knife until the mark became a sort of u or else a c and he decided to explain himself as best he could. I mean that if someone dies it's not like he stops existing, or at least not any more than he didn't exist before. Take nothingness for instance, if it exists it means that it really doesn't exist, that it's missing, but if it's missing it's been there or if it is what it isn't, it is in any case, in other words if nothingness exists it can't not exist, but you see? What else could a creature so hounded by existence do but stay constantly in movement? The mark that Jerzy had started to carve as a *c* had become a sort of S or like when an ∂ is attached to a *c* and so it looked like an *x*. So we are nothingness Sara concluded. Yes, but in the fourth dimension. The whole business was still unclear, but they decided to reflect on it further once they were dead.

And the trees twisted round and the foliage dipped up and down, the branches whipped back and forth and Sara came out of the tent with the sky low and cold and everything around was a frush shrish and a whoo whoorousssh. The trees were green and dark and their great boughs bent this way and that in the wind, and Sara knew that some were firs and others were oaks, names that no longer had a meaning, and there were hollow yews good for making bows and arrows too and if you trampled them and crushed them you could even make a poison to spread on the iron tips, and a single drop would be enough to put a child to sleep, and the belladonna was scattered on the ground by the storm, its dark berries nibbled by animals with stomach ailments or deer with the pain of a wound in their breast, and the earth was waterlogged and the mushrooms rotted on the ground and the worms crawled out too pale to escape the toads or birds and the hare would go to sleep in the rabbit holes, or in the dens of dogs or wolves, because that's what hares do. She climbed up to the rocks at the top of the rise that were still wet rocks, and stuck her fingers into the soggy earth that was still soggy earth, and wiped her face with her hand to get the rain off and it was still rain, and if she had to say how she felt she would have just said she felt, that she was, the way that Jerzy said dead people aren't. And her skin was cold, and her breath hot, her stomach empty and her teeth poking out of gums that could have bitten the air, ripped the rain away from the world, and she had thin, nervous hands, hands that could have fished Jerzy out of the mouths of mountains, out of ditches. She came back after the sun was down and slipped into the tent inside a sleeping bag patched with pieces of soft fur they had stretched, dried, softened with iron brushes and after a while she said that she had heard the trees talking, she had really heard them. What did they say? Wind. Wind? Wind.

They would wipe the water off their foreheads, and cheeks, and their jumpers were soaking wet, and the animal hides were rotting under the plastic tarps, and their eyes had grown big and shining, and they caressed each other behind the neck and knees and whispered promises or maybe just grazed each other with their breath. And Sara gave off a scent he had never smelled before, as if she was changing, as if she was turning into something else, something that had nothing to do with shivering and with the cold. And they made love so that Jerzy could see the vocal cords running through her breast and neck like razor blades. In the morning they saw nothing but steam slinking into their tent, into their nostrils, through the bark of the trees and when the fog rose from the ground, and swelled into a dense white cloud, then not even I could see things from up here, my gaze could reach neither Jerzy nor Sara. And it was then that it began to rain, for days on end, until an avalanche of mud came down the mountainsides as if the whole earth had become one big river and one big sound. Brrruuum.

V

— When I was a boy, anyway, as a kid. I was trying to do something but I fell asleep. There was a lawn, and I was running across it, there were other people with me running and then it's not that I fell down, I actually fell asleep. And I could see myself from the outside, you know what I mean? as if I were another person, but there was no other person. I could see myself asleep, that's all.
— Right.
— And then I was at school again, but school was in my house, in a room, and everyone around me was talking, and I was asleep. I saw myself asleep and said come on wake up dammit wake up .
— Horrible.
— Not really horrible, but yeah, there was something wrong.
— Were you afraid?
— Yes, I dunno, hold on, then I'm somewhere else, I'm on the tube, but the tube when it runs outside in the sun, not underground, you know? and so suddenly there are bombs falling, or there are people running, everyone's scared, we have to get out, we have to all go somewhere, but I go on sleeping, that is I see myself from the outside, and see I'm asleep and scream wake up and still I can't wake up. Then we're on a pebbly beach, maybe we got there by tube, I don't know, anyway I'm still

asleep, you're there too and you try to wake me up, but you
can't, you're crying or something. I'm asleep and hear
your voice but can't wake up, you're caressing my hair and face
or something and I can't wake up if you caress me but how
can I still go on sleeping if you're crying? so I hear you calling
someone, someone arrives, I hear noises, I can't open my
eyes, I'm going somewhere but can't see where, we're all going
somewhere as I sleep on but I don't understand where,
and you're caressing me and I can't wake up if you caress me.
I'm asleep and can't move any more, it's like my legs are
glued to something, or trapped in foam or in mud. I'm asleep
but not dreaming. Someone is pulling me, pushing me,
carrying me and I'm asleep. I'm asleep, after sleeping on the
lawn, at school, on the tube in the war, on the pebbly
beach, I'm asleep and I try to open my eyes, and when I open
them it's a huge effort, as if it hurt or something, but then
I open them and see I'm in a box, in a coffin, I was asleep, just
asleep and you all thought that I was dead.
— I haven't told her I'm pregnant.
— If you tell her she won't let us go.
— Don't talk rubbish, she's still my mother.
— You don't want to go anymore.
— Don't talk rubbish.
Jerzy gets out of bed, puts his right foot then his left on the ground.
He looks straight into the big mirror at the end of the room.
In it he can see Sara, who behind him, right behind him, is carefully
inspecting her hair. Jerzy lets his gaze slide from the smooth
surface of the mirror to the pillow where his head was resting, over
the folds of the sheets where he was lying.
— A sleeping man is like a closed box.
— What?
— You always think there's something inside.

VI

On the kitchen table are two glasses with orange juice in them,
two bowls full of cereal, a jug of milk, two containers of yoghurt, a pot
of coffee, nine slices of bread, three bananas and in the oven is
an apple cake. Jerzy opens the refrigerator, peers in, looks at the clock
over his head, peers into the refrigerator again, more intensely,
then turns around. Sara is drinking her orange juice slowly, sitting
with slumped shoulders, she gazes into the glass at the orange
oval moving towards her lips. Jerzy holds the refrigerator open with
one hand and peers into it even more intensely.
    — Yes, I'll freeze my bollocks off, I know you're thinking that
    I'll freeze my bollocks off like this, but I'm determined to find
    something she didn't think of.
    — Coffee?
    — She made another apple cake.
    — I made this one.
Jerzy comes away from the fridge and gets himself a slice of cake from
the oven, eating it in three bites. Outside the window from the sky to
the road it keeps raining.
    — It's raining.
    — At least here we have a house.
Jerzy looks out the window again at the rain, the road, a few dark
umbrellas, cars, headlights, yellow lights, above them the sun is just a
dingy, uniform light. Sara's mother must be somewhere in the city

doing charity work, getting kids off the streets, giving blankets to the homeless, squeezing orange juice in hospitals, giving mulled wine to alcoholics in the streets, rubbing alcohol over the naked, pale body of a man in a coma from an overdose, his skin sweating, his face green, his eyes yellow, hell is a dingy, uniform light. So it is above, so it is below.

Let the rain come,
the deluge, the black death,
the damp plague that blights everything.
Let death come,
death sitting astride
the virulent decaying dragon
with kerosene breath
that seeps everywhere and ignites without fire.
Let the sun go out,
let the earth turn to mud,
let the mud turn to water
let the night be bare of stars
and the moon stray
into the distant abyss
never to be seen again
in the long goodbye of the damp cold dark.
Let what I call come.
Let it come now,
Our sleep disturbs nothing
Our sleep disturbs nothing.
Our sweet sleep disturbs nothing.
Tomorrow, tomorrow
my brothers we will rise again
and to our warm blood
as always
we will bring the flame.

— Where does spring come back from when it comes back?
— What does spring have to do with anything?
— I mean that right now we're lying here, we're not even moving, soon we'll get up and the sun won't be there anymore, it will be dark, and none of this means that time has passed, or that there's anything like time that passes. All of this just means that we are on a planet that revolves around a star that is burning up, and that dusk is an astronomical report. We lie here and what we're wasting isn't time. We have the impression of time passing, but actually it's the earth covering distances, revolving and rolling around a sun that is itself moving in some direction, and then there's the spring that comes about when the sun is closer to us or when its rays hit us at a more perpendicular angle and your mother coming back from the hospital, and your mother's car has tyres of a certain diameter and thus a certain circumference like the earth, and to travel a mile those tyres must turn a certain number of times, but then there are also other cars other tyres, and it's this whole business of diameters and circumferences and bad drivers, it's all these relationships and nothing else that we call time. And that's the only reason why when your mother comes back it means it's late, it's evening . Look at that candle, it doesn't tell us time is passing, it just tells us the wax is burning up.

— Either you really can't stand my mother, or you had a lousy
time fucking just now.
— You remember the dog?
— The yellow one?
— Before they killed it, the people kicking it, and the more they
kicked it the more the dog ran and they had to run after it, run
around the pub.
— Those were people who'd lost all hope.
— That's what I mean. How long does it take to go a mile? it
depends on how long your legs are. But apart from that it's
a question of rage, or joy, or maybe you're bored, or sometimes
you get tired because a mile is still a mile.
— The business about the dog makes no sense at all.

Let every young father let go of his son's secret
Let his word be
Like the animal is to the den
Like the breast is to the mouth
Like the eye is to the prey

Let every young father let go of his son's dance
Let his hand be
Like the snow in winter
Like water is to the rock
Like these words of mine are to my tongue

Sing me the song
Let my ears listen to my mouth
Let my mouth be your hunger
Because I speak from the same hole I eat with
Let your food not be a ruse, let my speech not be a poison

Let my eye see the dark of the pupil in the ocean of my iris.

VIII

— How did they figure out that you have to get rid of the umbilical cord?

— Who?

— Men.

— What do men know about umbilical cords?

— Women, then.

— Mother dogs eat it, so do goats.

— Either by instinct or by experiment.

— You mean the first woman who had the first baby sat herself down to see what happened?

— Maybe.

— And?

— And the baby died.

— Let's say the first one dies because they don't know what they're supposed to cut off, and so they make another baby, wait nine months and when it comes out they cut its ears off.

— Why its ears?

— How do they know it's the cord that matters, are they studying the problem or aren't they?

— Or else they saw dogs eat it and so they ate it too.

— Maybe some things just happen, like breathing, like walking.

— I still wasn't walking at age two. Have you ever seen a whole umbilical cord or a placenta?

— Yes, maybe.
— It's this floppy thing that wraps around you and hangs
down from your belly, a thing that looks all wrong or like the
dead skin of a snake. Imagine a mother who sees herself
giving birth to something like a fish or a man inside an egg.
The first thing she'll do is pull away the scales, the rind,
until that thing in her hands looks like her, a human cub.
— Sort of like what you do in the mirror.
— What do you mean?
— I dunno, it makes me think of a mirror.
— It's just this whole business of a beginning that doesn't
add up.
— They ate it the way when you're little you eat your snot,
the scabs on your knees, your fingernails, sure, eating doesn't
have a beginning, it isn't something that starts, people have
always eaten. You know something though?
— What?
— The cord dries up and falls off naturally after three days,
there aren't any babies out there who die because no one's done
up their navel.
— That changes many things.

IX

— Maybe we should stop thinking that everything always starts over from the beginning.

The car drives through tunnels, across flyovers, slips along major thoroughfares, houses, trees, lawns, a river. They don't last long enough to be remembered, only the sky remains the sky and the road is always the only road. As he drives Jerzy's eyes are narrowed, his pupils slitted against the light of the cold white sun. Sara is wrapped up in a big blanket, her head tilted back to watch the sparkling clouds.

In the back they have cardboard boxes piled up on top of a metal chest and they have blankets and they've tanned and sewn together the hides to make a big tarpaulin and they have two shotguns and they have a bow and by now Jerzy would know how to make one with his hands if necessary, he'd know how to choose the right branch, how to pull off the unnecessary parts, how to stretch it like a scale. Through the windows they see a lake as big as a sea, and naked men running towards the water, and Jerzy says freezing and Sara says madmen, lunatics, and turns and sees them run into the water, amid patches of snow, one after the other like sea lions on the immobile, impassive lake.

It would be cold, Jerzy thinks, but they had already talked about that. They would dig a ditch in the ground they would put the tent in it and maybe cover it all up with tree branches or evergreens and snow on top of that but it wouldn't be for long, a month maybe two. And at night under the blankets he would make love to Sara and in the daytime, in the snow, he would do it with Sara who shivers more on one side than the other, and he would get them to give birth together in the cold so that he would have two babies that if you looked at them you'd say they're twins and if necessary they would make the stone by the river give birth too or any other part of the woods that he might have happened to inseminate even by mistake. Or else they would sleep in the car, or else they would make a tepee, three poles would be enough, in the days ahead he would add others, he would make a stove out of stones and earth, he had a spade and that was enough.

— You think jumpers were invented in the summertime?

— What?

— That's why we're going there, because you only think of water when you're thirsty .

— It works the other way around too, you think of water and then get thirsty .

— Mind letting me finish?

— Then finish.

— It's only when you're drinking that water and thirsty lose their meaning.

— That's all?

What was the point of taking planks of wood into a forest? They would cut down trees, pile logs on top of each other until they covered the sky, or even just made a roof or a bed out of spittle like bird nests, because you make things up like a recipe, you feel things in your tongue, on your palate. That a potato would go well with a chicken breast is something you can sense in your mouth without having known anything about it before. Because if you know how an orange tastes and how a duck tastes then some day it might dawn on you to put the two together and it might even all be a question of mistakes or even certitudes, and delays and errors and people who die of food poisoning, but then even their children and then their children's children would hold celebrations, Jerzy thinks.

They pass by women dressed in furs and men dressed in black drinking from steaming cups, and their mouths are steaming, and the street is steaming and up above a cloud breaks apart in the clear blue sky. And they pass by a sign that says welcome and right after it another one that says goodbye.

— There won't be much to eat.

— Yes there will, in winter things just get whiter and slower.

— Well, good.

The bear would be hibernating, half asleep, burping up fat, only getting up to piss every so often, at least that meant it would shut up for a while.

They overtake a car towing a boat, a mountain recedes behind them as they cross a bridge that vibrates in the emptiness, so high up that the clouds drift underneath.

Or else he would kill the bear, and it would grunt, bellow, spew blood instead of speaking and then he would eat it and make a rug out of it, but even in that state there was no way to be sure that the bear wouldn't be watching him from behind its glass eyes, and so he would make a flute out of its bones with as many holes as the fingers of a hand, and he would play it right and proper, the way you drive a car or a plane or something, and dances would be held among his people and maybe one day someone would come up with the idea of putting a stone inside the bear bone flute, or else an arrow, and the flute would become something else and then something else again.

— Maybe it will have had cubs.

— What?

— The bear.

— Since when is it female?

He has to take advantage of its hibernation, do everything possible, the she-bear will wake up to find a new world, and even without a bear-bone flute his children's children will dance, because nothing can stop the celebration.

They drive through a countryside patched with dark, snow-mottled fields. Transparent greenhouses shaped like grubs and others shaped like tubes, cylinders, the sun following them reflected on the translucent surfaces and aluminium arches.

For the feast of thieves anyone could steal from anyone, carry away any object, pick it up, put it in their pockets, in total secrecy, with the dexterity and skill of a real thief. No clumsiness or bluster would be allowed, only pure theft. The only restriction would be that you had to know every detail of the object before you could even think about stealing it. Know its materials, its history and who figured in it. Only then would you have the sacred right to swipe it, nick it, steal it. The second time around no one will go looking for what was stolen from them the year before, what point would there be?

— Then they'll want the feast of lunatics, of cuckolds, of murderers.

— Those are variations, just like you can steal someone else's woman you can take his life.

They pass by a cemetery, they pass by a neon sign showing a palm tree, the crown pink the trunk flashing electric blue, two yellow coconuts flashing as well, then the shopping centre.

At each new birth a mouthful of meat would be cut away. The whole community would eat it. Every year on the person's birthday the operation would be repeated. This ritual, aside from making every individual responsible for his or her good health, would provide the community with new yardsticks of judgement. Men and women would no longer be just beautiful, kind, wise, or crass, they would be salty, sweet, tender, or bitter, or too fat or stringy. Nothing would be more gratifying than hearing someone say this shank of yours is delicious, can I have some more?

And the foetus in Sara's belly hears the sound that a stomach makes and the sound of air in the lungs and cascades of water in the oesophagus, it opens and closes its fingers and in its larynx it has all it needs to emit the first sound but it stretches out something like a leg.

— It just moved.

Or else men who live only in caves, pale, hairless, fluorescent as fish in the depths, their children transparent as jellyfish. And these men would be the only sources of light, and the rocks and walls of the cave, and the stalactites and stalagmites and clumps of lime would all take on a shape when the men's luminous bodies approached, the rest of the world would fall back into darkness and be forgotten, or else to trace the layout of the cave they would have to move forward in pairs.

They pass by a frozen canal, a frozen pool, a frozen lake, children, men, manikins and women in red and grey and mustard-coloured jackets skate on it, slip, fall, a thin black figure does a pirouette.

   — Are there still fish underneath?

   — Of course.

   — I mean it's strange to think about, isn't it?

   — What?

   — How you're there skating, having fun, right over a lake, and underneath maybe there are fish that have no idea that you're there having fun.

   — I think they know.

Or else a society where people are not taught to sleep, they don't know anything about it. Since they don't know how to sleep, they would work, eat, kill, fuck until they passed out. And along with sleep, dreams would be unknown. A society like that would believe life was continuous, and sleep would be confused with waking, there would be no division between the worlds of daytime and night-time, or the worlds of outside and inside, everything would be forever. And men working on a fence would dream that they'd finished it and in the morning it would still be skeletal, but they wouldn't care because for sleepless men things repeat themselves, and all metaphysics would disappear forever.

   — As a little girl I used to go sledding on a plastic bag down the hill in front of my house.

   — We've all sledged down hills on plastic bags, there's nothing better.

   — Then my clothes would be all wet.

   — That's the only problem with snow-covered hills.

Or else a society where the first person singular pronoun was never heard. She would ask do you love the person in front of you? He would answer the person in front of you loves you. Or else they would all speak only in the third person, no one would feel confused and panicked, it would always, only happen to someone else, death would no longer be able to touch us, it would always, only come for someone else. Maybe, Jerzy thinks, it would be a race of warriors who felt no pain, martyrs willing to let themselves be skinned alive, suicide brigades prepared to blow themselves up in supermarkets, cinemas, tube stations, everything that happened would actually happen to someone else, to a him or a her who is never a me.

Or else a race of poets, a race that could sing of their roots, their father, their mother. Or else only a poet would be taught to sing, or else his ears would be cut off, torn away, boiled, his eardrums cooked so he could no longer hear, learn, let himself be confused by new songs, songs from across the border, and for his brothers alone the poet would repeat the notes of the observance.

> *Born from a rock,*
> *fecundated by a fisherman*
> *with the buttocks of a bear, and the head of a man,*
> *long before the brambles ever rose,*
> *before the border of the world was traced,*
> *before silence was imposed.*

Jerzy closes his eyes, tries to sleep, the white fluorescent line of the road runs in front of them, the darkness has swallowed up all the rest, only the faint gleam of the snow and a few lights from far-off houses tell him that the world still exists. Sara grips the wheel resolutely, there's a piano playing in the car, Jerzy lets his head fall back.

And the son would couple with the mother and the son's daughter with the father, or else the women would give birth in hollow trees, so that the son would be said to be born from the wood itself. Or else a society of butchers capable of sticking a human foetus into the womb of a dog, a deer, a goat, into the rubbery belly of a toad. Or else a society where children are suckled by swine and by wolves, never by women. Or else the truth would be accepted as a lie, and you could be the child of the poplar tree one day and the child of the wolf the next and things would always be in movement like saying that the moon is a woman and you're never sure when it's happy because sometimes it will be sad, sometimes beautiful, sometimes tired and sometimes pregnant.

— At twenty below people freeze to death.

— Even before that, are you afraid?

— A little.

— Good.

Or else death would come bit by bit, people's ears would die first and their eyes last. Someone would see his left leg dying then his right, never all together and so he would be able to say goodbye to himself, say goodbye like when you sail out to sea and the coastline disappears or when you get undressed, first your trousers then your underpants.

    — I don't know about dying but your fingers can always freeze, they turn blue then transparent, like ice or cobalt, then all it takes is one blow and thock, they come right off, in pieces.

    — And if you don't touch them till summer?

Or else like dogs, men would creep away to die in secret, in caves, or in ditches in the ground, and there would be no word that meant death, or else the word would be forget. People would be forgotten. What happened to Jerzy? He forgot to come by. Or a society where a father does not know the son of his son, and the number of individuals could never be more than three. The son would wait for his father's death to sleep with his mother, and the daughter would give birth to her father's daughter only after killing her mother and so on. Jerzy runs one hand through his hair, takes Sara's in his own, kisses it delicately, turns right smoothly at the junction, an idea like that was like being immortal.

    — But what if we need something?

    — Like what?

    — Like a hospital, a doctor, a house, a road.

    — Those already exist everywhere, who needs them anymore.

    — You promised.

    — I promised.

They would avoid uttering the word time, they would also avoid waiting, or even being late or worse yet being early, until time was gone, because time was only a distance and so they would just cut it short, take shortcuts. And when they lay in ambush for game, what they felt in their bones or in their skin would not be time passing, it would be the sun warming them or the morning dew drenching their arse. Without time no one would have killed yesterday to be punished tomorrow.

The car runs along the road that cuts through snow-covered fields. Sara is drinking from a can of Coke.

— You think this will be good for the baby?

— Have you asked it?

Sara's hands are pale and healthy, her belly sticking out proud and arrogant now and Jerzy has forgotten the wheel in his hands and the road in front of him and the fields of snow as well, he's thinking of a rule, just one, just one rule, a law that would eradicate all bureaucracies. He arrives at that law a few curves later, a simple law, because it is in simplicity that beauty lies, and his rule is beautiful or at least so it seems to him. His law could be applied to everyone, without exception. There would be no lawyers to find loopholes, introduce flaws, and breaking it would be senseless. At every new birth they would take out all the child's baby teeth and then do the same when adult ones grew in. No one would be able to bite, take, divide, hash, shred, turn everything into a detail, you could only suck things whole. Jerzy imagines himself coming back to the camp after a day of hunting, or after foraging for plants, a motley swarm of children running to meet him, their arms stretched up and their mouths open in grimaces of joy, dark and irredeemably toothless holes, O. Jerzy plunges into another curve and the road opens up into a long straight line that seems to gently rise into the cold blue sky. The teeth would have to stay, Jerzy thinks, there will simply be no biting allowed, things can only be swallowed. Only sucked at. Sucking has nothing to do with breathing, nothing. Sucking is even more ancient, Jerzy thinks, and he thinks of bridges, and then he thinks of gravity, and dwarf stars and white ones and the universe like a diaphragm, pockets of emptiness sucking up the fullness. And so Jerzy comes to the conclusion that sucking is more devastating than biting, more destructive than chewing, sucking now brings to mind something that has to do with origins, but not of children, babies, toothless creatures.

— Sucking is worse than the big bang.

— What?

— No sucking allowed, from childhood on.

Sara runs a hand over Jerzy's thin face, then turns towards the white silent fields.

— Camilla's a nice name.

— If it's a girl we'll call her Camilla.

And so they would give the name Camilla to everything, to the trees of course, but also to the rocks, the pools, the frogs. Camilla was the clouds, Camilla was hair, Camilla was feet, Camilla was the ducks that come in summer and the ones that leave in winter, Camilla was the firewood and the planks for making houses and Camilla was also the branches of brambles and the thorns and that burning pain when they scratch you. So when his children had a multitude of things in front of them, the whole multitude of the world, every difference would be erased, everything would be a single being and there would be no more questions to ask, everything would be Camilla, his children themselves would no longer think they were different from anything else, because they too would all be named Camilla, all of them without regard for sex, because even that, the penis would be called Camilla and the cunt Camilla as well.

— Camilla is nice.

This would also solve the problem of the nights without names. By the side of the road a boy is holding a horse by its bridle, one hand turning its head away, they pass by, Sara makes a gesture like a wave, the horse is dappled.

Or else children that become adults in the cradle, that grow up in just one night as they sleep, in the morning the cradle is lying there in pieces and on top of it is a woman or man and you have to wake them up, Jerzy thinks. The luckier ones will remember their dreams, they'll all lend a hand with the work to be done.

In the snow-covered fields Sara sees crystalline tracks of bird feet, dark green trees, a ripped-up fence, the leafless brambles covered in frost like breath frozen in the air and fallen to earth, she opens the window and the air is cold.

— It smells good.

On the road in front of them two men in a snowplough nod to them from the rear-view mirrors, Jerzy slows down, the lights on top of the plough are yellow and orange, the big steel blade heaps the snow at the edges of the road spread with salt.

A Society that Breathes Once a Year
Alex Cecchetti

This publication is published
as part of *The Time Machine*,
commissioned by Book Works
and Francesco Pedraglio from
open submission

Published and distributed
by Book Works

Commissioning editor:
Francesco Pedraglio

Edited by Gavin Everall and
Francesco Pedraglio

Translated by Johanna Bishop

Proofreading by Gerrie van Noord

Designed by Atelier Dreibholz:
Paulus M. Dreibholz and
Daniel McGhee

Printed by Die Keure, Bruges

Copyright © Alex Cecchetti, 2012.
All rights reserved. No part of
this publication may be reproduced,
copied or transmitted save with
written permission from the publi-
shers or in accordance with the
provisions of the Copyright Designs
and Patents Act, 1988

ISBN 978 1906012 32 8

Book Works
19 Holywell Row
London EC2A 4JB
www.bookworks.org.uk
tel: +44(0)20 7247 2203

Book Works is funded by Arts
Council England, and this
publication was made possible
with the support of the French
Embassy in the UK

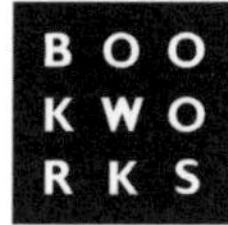

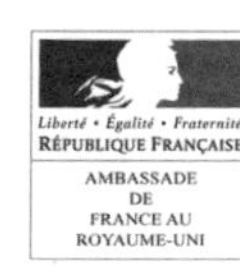

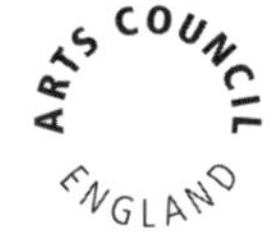

Photo Styling

How to Build Your Career
and Succeed

Susan Linnet Cox

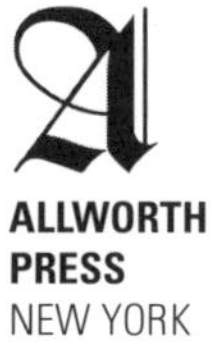

ALLWORTH
PRESS
NEW YORK

Published by Allworth Press
An imprint of Allworth Communications, Inc.
10 East 23rd Street, New York, NY 10010

Cover design by Derek Bacchus
Interior design by Dianna Little
Typography by SR Desktop Services, Ridge, NY
Cover photograph by Michael Christmas

ISBN: 1-58115-452-6

Library of Congress Cataloging-in-Publication Data
Cox, Susan Linnet.
   Photo styling : how to build your career and succeed / Susan Linnet Cox.
        p.   cm.
   Includes index.
   1. Photography—Vocational guidance.   2. Image consultants—
Vocational guidance.   3. Fashion.   I. Title.
TR154.C69   2006
770.23—dc22
                                                    2006013940

Printed in Canada